HENRY·NEWBOLT

and
The SPIRIT of CLIFTON

HENRY·NEWBOLT
and
The SPIRIT *of* CLIFTON .

Derek Winterbottom

'Spiritus intus Alit'

To speak of Fame a venture is,
    There's little here can bide,
But we may face the centuries,
    And dare the deepening tide:
For though the dust that's part of us
    To dust again be gone,
Yet here shall beat the heart of us
    The School we handed on!

REDCLIFFE
Bristol

First published in 1986
by Redcliffe Press Ltd.,
49 Park St., Bristol.

© Derek Winterbottom

ISBN 0 948265 80 9

Typeset by Folio Photosetting, Bristol
Printed by WBC Print Ltd.

CONTENTS

LIST OF ILLUSTRATIONS

Illustrations numbered 1, 2, 3, 4, 5, 6, 13, 14, 16, 19 and 21 are reproduced by courtesy of Mr Peter Newbolt; number 15, Thomas-Photos of Oxford and number 18, Wilts. County Council Library Service. The front cover photograph was taken by Mr G.P. Rendle. The remainder are from the Clifton College Archives.

PREFACE

It shocks me to remember, in 1986, that my experience of Clifton now reaches back nearly twenty years. I was captivated then, as I still am, by the sights and sounds of the place, and my interest in Newbolt stems not least from the feeling that in this respect he was a kindred spirit. In 1983 a lucky chance brought me to meet Dr Richard Hitchcock at an O.C. gathering in Devon, and he offered most generously to place on permanent loan in the Percival Library his very extensive collection of Newbolt's works. This gesture not only enriched the Library but gave me easy access to my source material. I have also been encouraged greatly by Mr Peter Newbolt who, with his wife Marcia, has done all he can to help, not only by granting permission to quote from his grandfather's works but also by providing information and lending some splendid family photographs for repro-duction in this book. Most of the writing was done in my parents' house on the Isle of Man, and I thank them for their hospitality and for lending an ear to readings of the text as it gradually appeared. The typing of the manuscript was undertaken by a serving Cliftonian in Watson's House who with his associates manipulated the College's recently-installed word processor laboriously yet to good effect: Newbolt, a great supporter of technological advance, would surely have approved. The sharp eyes of my colleague Geoffrey Hardyman scanned the text for solecisms and I am grateful for his time and trouble. When I started on this book Newbolt meant not really much more than a name and a song to me. As I came, through his work, to know him better, my admiration and respect for his literary skills steadily increased. I only hope that the contrast in this book between his words and mine is not too marked.

D.O.W.
Clifton, March 1986.

PART ONE: 1862–1876

'All men are poets, especially in childhood'

'I was born in June 1862, that is in the same year and even the same month in which the School itself came into existence. You will recognise that this coincidence gives me a unique position, the position of It, the Absolute: or at least it makes me, like the speed of light, the one permanent unit of computation. It identifies me mentally with the School; whatever at any moment is past to the School is past also to me: what is future to the School is future to me.' [1] On a summer's evening, sixty years after the twin births referred to in his speech, Sir Henry Newbolt, newly elected President of the Old Cliftonian Society made this declaration in Big School at a supper for young and old Cliftonians. For one who had during his life become conscious of being above all else a traveller in Time it was doubtless a poignant moment and one of which he sought to make his audience aware. 'I must tell you this, gentlemen, that although we enjoy every moment of these visits to you at Commemoration, and though you see us laughing and talking gaily enough, we cannot be here without profound emotions — our very gaiety is partly a cover to hide them — and we greatly desire that you should understand and sympathise with us in this. It is no easy matter: you do not know the world as we know it, your view is relative, you see from one point of view only, where we see from two. We, but not you, spent most of the years of our life under the influence of two expectations, two convictions. We had the certainty that our Country must pass through the trial of a great European war; much of our effort we spent in preparing for it, some in military training, some of us in preparation of the heart. We had also the certainty that Clifton by her natural destiny must become one of the greatest of English schools. That was an act of faith, for in actual achievement the Clifton of our time was almost incredibly different from the Clifton you know.'

Indeed, it was. By 1922 the 'Great Game' was over, visions had been shattered, idols destroyed, new plans made. The guns of criticism had been turned, since 1918, on many previously accepted assumptions. *The Cliftonian* magazine for March 1920 had printed a poem of five verses which ended

9

Then let us pluck up courage and make complaint to those
who make us carry rifles and wear these khaki clothes,
For since we have all these parades we only hate the more
That ancient institution — the Clifton College Corps.[2]

The times, and the mood, had certainly changed. Loyalty, Patriotism, Chivalry, dreams of ambition and imperial service, all that Henry Newbolt had sought to advance through the printed word were suddenly suspect virtues. He had become a national figure because he had once been able to express the popular mood through poetry. But this was 1922 and even as he succeeded to the Presidency of the Old Cliftonian Society, the 'Newbolt era' was ending. He doubtless knew it. He was not — as a superficial glance at his most quoted work might suggest to some — a limited jingoist, a simple sportsman, a sentimental mediocrity. His was a bright intellect and it centred, as a poet's should, on Truth and Time. Yet he needed anchors in the real world and the most solid of these was his experience of Clifton College.

Though born in the same year as Henry Newbolt, Clifton College lay longer conceiving. A group of influential Bristol citizens had met in April 1860 to found a Limited Company to raise share capital for the building of a Public School in the City[3]. A twelve acre site was purchased next to the Zoological gardens in Clifton and the designs of Charles Hansom were selected for the buildings. The most vital decision to be made was the choice of Headmaster. Canon John Guthrie for the Council of the new College approached Dr. Frederick Temple, Headmaster of Rugby School, seeking his advice. Rugby was at that time the most influential of the Public Schools because it was the place which Thomas Arnold had made great and famous by his reforming zeal. Here the potentially idle and errant young were fashioned into Christian gentlemen and it was precisely this mixture of religion and gentility that appealed strongly to the founders of Clifton College, as indeed it appealed to so many members of the Victorian middle classes. Temple recommended the Rev. Charles Evans, a much respected senior master at Rugby, and in March 1861 the news of his appointment as Headmaster of Clifton was released. 'His brilliant University career and deeply religious character, together with his great experience and success as a teacher and as a master, eminently qualify Mr. Evans for this important office', the Council proudly announced.[4] The opening day was fixed for September 9th 1862; work on Big School and School House went according to plan and a preliminary school was set up to collect a few boys for the opening. Then within days of his scheduled arrival at Clifton, the Headmaster resigned.

'The retirement of the Rev. Charles Evans from the Head-mastership occasioned the Council more anxiety than they can adequately express'[5] the official report stated, more than hinting at the consternation and panic that probably seized the Council and shareholders. A lot of money was at stake: public confidence had to be maintained at all costs. Evans had decided to accept the Head Mastership of King Edward VI's Grammar School in Birmingham, his old school, a flourishing and ancient foundation. To put it mildly this was a controversial decision and it left the Council desperate. A number of names were considered but Dr. Temple lent his support to a very young man who had been on his staff at Rugby only two years, apparently promising that if he were appointed he would do for Clifton what Arnold had done for Rugby.[6] It was a dreadful risk: a brilliant examinee at Oxford, John Percival had nonetheless suffered nervous breakdowns; he was only just 28 and on the point of marriage, he had only two years' experience of teaching the lower forms at Rugby and, springing from unpretentious farming stock in Westmorland whose accents he retained with pride, he did not seem the obvious choice to create a school with high social aspirations. Until, that is, the interview. Face to face with him the Council were presumably struck, as thousands were after them, by the quiet power of his presence and were moved to take the biggest gamble of their corporate lives. Evans' resignation was announced on September 4th whereupon the Council reported that 'The Rev. John Percival M.A., Fellow of Queen's College, Oxford, who has added to a career of almost unsurpassed brilliancy at that University the experience of two years' mastership at Rugby, is now the Head Master, and the Council have obtained such satisfactory testimonials to his fitness for the position that they regard the College as eminently fortunate in securing his services'.[7]

The formal opening of Clifton College took place on September 30th 1862, by which time Henry Newbolt already lay three months old in his Staffordshire vicarage cot. He would have been embarrassed to have this pointed out to him at the Clifton dinner sixty years later when he claimed that both he and the School were born in June: he was a great advocate of accuracy in detail. On that opening day, beneath the lofty and elegant gables of Charles Hansom's Tudor Gothic Big School, addressing an audience of some seventy boys and a large concourse of well-wishers John Percival preached his first Clifton sermon, and an expectant audience heard for the first time the compelling Westmorland tones of the voice that was to mesmerize Cliftonians for the next seventeen years. Newbolt described it later in his autobiographical novel *The Twymans*: 'The printed record of his sermons or his speeches could scarcely tell more to a reader who had never known the living voice, than the score of a sonata could convey its moving power to one unskilled in music. But the instrument once heard, the bare notation will suffice to bring back the full sound to memory: Percy could never afterwards read a line of these brief and unadorned utterances without seeing instantly and with the clearness of life the tall spare figure, the chiselled face, with its lofty and remote air, saved from too dominant an austerity by the grace of the slightly stooping head: or without hearing again in every sentence the lingering north-country accent that gave so curious a distinction to the voice, and the unconsciously melancholy cadence that softened its strenuousness with a grave beauty of resignation'.[8] On this occasion Percival spoke, naturally, of the great responsibilities they all shared, of the need for resolution, and prayer: 'If you desire to belong to a place of which you may be justly proud; if you wish to hear this College spoken of as one that bears a high name as a place where truth and uprightness and purity and all Christian virtues are held in honour; as a place where all that is base or unworthy is hated and despised, — then remember that it rests with you to give it that name'.[9] Here, from the very first day was the spirit that would over the years mould from those boys a great and flourishing school; a spirit pure Percival, pure Newbolt.

There can be no doubt that as a Headmaster, Percival was a pheno-menon. He had a marvellous opportunity at Clifton, and he made the very most of it. The school started with 76 boys. When Percival left in 1879, there were 680. This fact alone is most remarkable when a comparison is made with other schools of both ancient and new foundation which struggled to attract boys during the same period. The point is that Percival was not just an impressive sermoniser and exponent of high moral tone; he had shrewd, practical, northern common sense that made him an excellent organiser and business man. Moreover he was not afraid of appointing teachers of outstanding ability to his staff, for he knew he could inspire and control them. His first appointment, Graham Dakyns, stayed twenty-seven years and was a profound influence on the school. So were Thomas Brown the Manx poet, who served Clifton for 30 years, Edward Oakeley, George Wollaston, Sydney Irwin and Norman Moor. Newbolt was to know them well.

Henry John Newbolt was born on June 6th 1862 in St. Mary's Vicarage, Baldwin Street, Bilston, Staffordshire. His father, the Rev. Henry Francis

Newbolt, was vicar of the parish: his grandfather, Captain Charles Newbolt had served in Nelson's fleet. His mother, born Emily Stubbs, was his father's second wife and came from a Staffordshire business family with Jewish connections. The population of the Black Country town of Bilston had grown to 16,000 in the 1820's and it was thought necessary to build another church in addition to the medieval St. Leonard's. Designed in the Georgian Gothic style St. Mary's was consecrated in 1830 though the porous stone of which the church was constructed soon became discoloured by soot and dust from the surrounding chimneys and furnaces. Newbolt recalled that 'the walks of my childhood were treeless and smoke-blighted: they led me by black canals and among huge slag-heaps where no grass could grow, where the sun rarely shone, where at night a man could read his newspaper by the glare of the blast furnaces, luridly reflected in the dense low sky.'[10] A cholera epidemic swept through the town in 1832 causing 742 deaths and leaving 450 children orphaned. A tablet in the vestry of St. Mary's underlines the health hazards of those times. It reads 'In memory of Joseph, son of Joseph and Mary Ann Meek, who was accidentally drowned in the cistern of the Day School adjoining this church, April 30 1845 aged 8 years. This distressing event is recorded by the minister as an expression of sympathy with the parents and caution to the children of the school, a reproof to the proprietors of open pits, wells and landslips, the want of fencing about which is the frequent cause of similar disaster in these districts, and as a momento to all of the uncertainty of life, and the consequent necessity of immediate and continued preparation for death.' It was fifteen years after this tragedy that the Rev. Henry Newbolt was appointed to the parish, in 1860. He and his wife lived at the Vicarage until his early death six years later, and there were born three children, Henry, Francis and Emily. He was a popular preacher and lecturer, a strong Anglican Churchman yet with many friends among the Quakers and Wesleyans. His death at the age of 42 plunged his widow into a lengthy period of grief, though her four-year-old eldest child had not known his father well or long enough to share her sorrows fully. The parishioners certainly realised their loss: a monument in the church was erected by 'many who loved him among his deeply attached people and sorrowing friends in grateful acknowledgement of the grace given unto him to preach among them the unsearchable riches of Christ and to set before them an example of Christian charity, piety and zeal in his master's service during the six years of his ministry here.'

The widow and her three young children left St. Mary's Vicarage and moved to Walsall where the Stubbs family had long been prominent in the town. The dominating influence was Grandfather Stubbs, a man of business and strong character who had, it was said, retired from his various occupations in disgust at the passing of the Great Reform Bill forty years before. His death in 1873 left Mrs. Newbolt and her sisters comfortably endowed. Newbolt had happy memories of these Walsall years. 'The place was not beautiful, but it was well inhabited and well neighboured — we had many friends in the town and outside, and though too few of them were young like ourselves, there were among them a number who were delightful companions for the young'.[11] There were holidays, too, in the Malvern Hills, in Yorkshire and in North Wales and it was now that he developed an interest in birdwatching and fishing — both to remain lifelong hobbies. At the age of ten years, however, there was the matter of formal education to be considered. The Second Master of Queen Mary's Grammar School in Walsall had given the willing Newbolt tuition three times a week and recommended that he should be coached for an Eton Scholarship at a suitable preparatory school. He and his brother Frank were therefore sent to Caistor in Lincolnshire where Anthony Bower who had tutored Newbolt's father at Cambridge had been appointed Headmaster of the Grammar School. 'Newbolt', he said, 'I wonder if you will be as good a pupil as your father was. He *was* a sharp fellow — one of the sharpest I ever taught.'[12]

It was an unconventional school. There was little organisation outside lessons and the boys were free to explore the surrounding Lincolnshire Wolds. 'I am sure that we gained greatly from our informal wanderings in that wide and idyllic landscape. Here, though the hills were mostly bare and the fields not always sunlit, we were unconsciously affected by the character of the country — it was consistent and immemorial, in a word bucolic. We learnt much about reaping and rick-building and the edible qualities of swedes, and a good deal more about rams and lambs than boys in orthodox schools can ever know.'[13] The countryside, especially its timeless qualities, had a lifelong appeal for Newbolt and his feeling for it was certainly quickened by his experience of Caistor. 'To Percy, with only ten years behind him, and the smoke of great towns hanging closely over all the fields of his experience, it was just the wide high loneliness that made the joy of it. For four years his feet wandered that country with a delight as fresh as morning: and after thirty more had gone by the recollection of it still lay upon his imagination like an enchantment.'[13] Of course, in many respects Caistor was like other schools: there were petty rivalries, pecking orders, fights and visitations of the cane. But young Newbolt enjoyed the earthiness of it and savoured the Lincolnshire dialect of Tennyson's *Northern Farmer*, a poet's sensibilities already wide awake. Above all there was in the local church the cross-legged effigy of a fighting man, believed to be a thirteenth century Crusader. Here was an emphatic yet mysterious symbol of Chivalry, the theme that was to dominate Newbolt's life and work, recurrent in his poems, novels, speeches, thought and action.

PART TWO: 1876–1881

'Your heart is with Clifton and the accidents of your own life.'
H.G.Wells to Henry Newbolt, 1904

It was surely a compliment to John Percival's sucess that Anthony Bower determined to send his promising pupil to sit the scholarship examination not, after all, at Eton but at Clifton. Now aged fourteen Henry Newbolt travelled down to Bristol with another boy, marvelling at the 'rich warm radiance of the west.' From Temple Meads station they took a cab across the centre of the City, a bustling port in those days, uphill through Georgian Clifton and towards the College. The whole area had been for ten years and more the scene of vigorous building activity. Newly planned streets had been filled with handsome villas, most with vast bow-fronted drawing rooms that promised elegance and fine living. The College itself, distanced from these buildings by the playing field named, Rugby-fashion, 'The Close' had grown magnificently in fourteen years. Canon Guthrie had died in 1865 and, aware of the Headmaster's feelings about the central importance of religion in the school, Mrs. Guthrie offered to build a Chapel as a memorial to her husband: it was opened in 1867. Three years later the 'Percival Library' buildings were completed, the gift of the Headmaster, and in 1876 the Junior School was added, just in time for Newbolt's arrival. It was not quite the architectural cluster of today; there was no Wilson Tower, no East Cloister; nor had the group developed in exactly the way the architect had first envisaged. Yet Clifton College was a very fine sight and his first view of boys playing cricket on the Close in June made the sort of unforgettable impression upon Henry Newbolt that it has doubtless made on many Cliftonians since. Not all have expressed it so memorably: 'as he drew level and looked between the trees he saw that which took his breath with an entirely new delight. In the distance were buildings — in front lay a wide green sward, level as a lawn, flooded with low sunlight, and covered in every direction with a multitude of white figures, standing, running, walking, bowling, throwing, batting — in every attitude that can express the energy or the expectancy of youth.'[1] Newbolt passed the examination, which was just as well, for in the week he had spent at Clifton he had fallen in love with the place.

Towards the end of his life John Percival, by then Bishop of Hereford, distributed the prizes at Whitgift, a London day school, and announced that 'his experience at Clifton led him to the conclusion that the best education in English life was not to be had in a boarding school, but was obtained by the boy who lived in a good home and attended a good school near his home.'[2] One of the most original features of Percival's Clifton was the large day boy element assembled in the Town House, divided in 1875 into North Town and South Town. Mrs. Newbolt, persuaded no doubt by a mixture of the educational advantages, the attractiveness of the suburb and the desire to enjoy the company of her family decided to live in Clifton and accordingly bought a house in Worcester Crescent, overlooking the College and the Close. Both Henry and Francis Newbolt were therefore day boys throughout their five years at school while their younger sister Milly was a day pupil at Clifton High School for Girls, which lay even nearer to the family home than the College.

As Newbolt lingers in the popular mind as a man who promoted and glorified the Victorian Public School, it is worth pausing to reflect whether he would have enjoyed life at Clifton quite so much as a boarder. In his comfortable home and in the absence of a father he doubtless played the man about the house, enjoying also the devoted attention of his mother and his sister, 'a glowing Cinderella, a voluntary — or more than half voluntary — fag of all work. She attended the boys before their departure to school, with boots, caps, and notebooks, and again, on their return, with slippers, buttered toast, and consolation for the troubles of the day.'[3] Not for him the jungle of a boarding house where, it might be said, the true character-building takes place. It is remarkable how many men of literary and artistic tastes have loathed their Public Schools and vilified them afterwards in print; their independent and perhaps original natures not responding well to the submission of self required by the system. Even Newbolt's Clifton contemporaries Arthur Quiller-Couch and Roger Fry had major reservations. On the other hand Newbolt had enjoyed the knockabout tribal warfare of his preparatory school and knew what it was like to live away from home. Civilised and sensitive he might have been, but soft in any sense he was not.

In his 1922 speech Newbolt had said that the Clifton of the 1870's was 'almost incredibly different' from the post-war school and indeed the earlier period had already begun to take on a legendary glow, so that it is not always easy to disentangle truth from fiction. To some extent this resulted from literary outpourings of a reminiscent nature, one of the first of which was Francis Newbolt's *Clifton College 25 years ago, The Diary of a*

Fag published in 1904. Neither this nor its sequel *The Diary of a Praepostor* published fifteen years later shows Newbolt minor to be from the same literary stable as his brother, but both books are interesting sources of information. Macmillan published *The Collected Poems of T.E. Brown* in 1909 and William Temple, the future Archbishop of Canterbury, wrote the official *Life of Bishop Percival* in 1921, as befitted a dutiful and admiring godson. J.R. Mozley, who spent a year as a member of staff in the 1860s, lionized some of his more prominent contemporaries in *Clifton Memories*, 1927, and this was soon followed by O.F. Christie's *Clifton Schooldays, 1879–1885*. Newbolt himself produced not only the Clifton poems but his autobiographical novel *The Twymans* and eventually *My World as in my Time*, a first volume of memoirs published in 1932. For all these authors, Percival was an idol beyond reproach, many of the masters were teachers of genius, many of the boys went on to pursue careers of great distinction, the atmosphere and tone of the place was almost without blemish, the forces of Destiny had clearly found a permanent site in 'the best School of all'. Can this really be true?

Given the Lytton Strachey treatment even Percival might be made to look slightly absurd, especially in the years after Clifton. As President of Trinity he was too much of a disciplinarian for the tastes of many undergraduates, and Newbolt remembered seeing in an Oxford shop-window 'the scandalous caricatures of Percival as a sandwich man . . . photographically lifelike, pungently humorous'.[4] The placards, of course, advertised some unwelcome regulation Percival had introduced. And as Headmaster of Rugby (in his last year admittedly) he took against bare knees on the games field and ordained that elastic bands should be fitted to keep shorts reaching down to stockings. When Bishop of Hereford, moreover, there were those who felt that Percival's interest in Liberal theology was more suited to an urban rather than a rural diocese.[5] Even at Clifton his accent must have caused amusement, as in his objection to 'law tawn' and his famous remonstrance 'Dawn't live the life of a cabbage maan!'.[6] 'Jumps' and 'John Perkeye' the boys called him. As Newbolt observed, 'Boys have an instinctive resistance to doctrine — they use their sense of humour to ensure themselves against too much eloquence or idealism. The school resisted Percival — to a point.'[7] There were plenty, too, one suspects, who dozed through his sermons: boys simply do not change that much from one decade to the next. Yet anecdotes such as these cannot possibly disguise the fact that by sheer force of personality and weight of achievement Percival was a living legend to all who knew him, not least to Henry Newbolt, for whom 'he was the most satisfying figure of a great man that could be found or imagined — he had the grace of a marble statue; not a gesture was free, and yet he was seen to move perfectly. In our Roman world he was a being apart, a form with the crystallised perfection of the Greek art.'[8]

What of the masters? Percival's biographer William Temple, himself a former headmaster, wrote 'No part of a headmaster's duty is more important than the selection of his assistants; here Percival was supreme. He cared comparatively little for technical qualifications but had an unerring eye for individuality and character. His Clifton staff was one of the most brilliant ever gathered together at a single school.'[9] Francis Newbolt, the reverse of sentimental, wrote more bluntly. 'I thought many of the (masters) eccentric, and the years have not modified this view, but on the other hand what magnificent teachers some of them were.'[10] 'For certain', wrote Sir Arthur Quiller-Couch, 'a high proportion of these Clifton masters were 'characters'. Indeed, it is hardly too much too say that we boys considered most of them to be more than a little mad; suspected even that John Percival ... had chosen and collected his staff for their various eccentricities, wisely, because while they made teaching vivid, provocative, amusing, he could always control them to a common purpose and tradition. Under that compelling will of his, backed in some measure by irascibility, masters and boys had so conspired to plant and foster tradition that within twenty years of its foundation the ethos of Clifton had rooted itself as firmly as though Clifton had stood for centuries.'[11]

Percival appointed 91 men to his staff, eleven of whom left to pursue distinguished careers in Universities, four of them gaining election as Fellows of the Royal Society. About a dozen left to become Headmasters and another dozen to run Anglican parishes: the most remarkable characters, however, seem to have been among those who stayed at Clifton.

The names one hears most frequently are those of Dakyns, Brown, Oakeley, Dunn, Wollaston, Moor, and Irwin: they are remembered chiefly because they were all men of wide intellectual interests, whose horizons extended well beyond Clifton and who delighted in introducing to like-minded boys the cultural pleasures they themselves held dear. This was perhaps an easier task a hundred years ago than it might be today because school life then was far less varied. The curriculum, even at Clifton, was a narrow one, still relying very heavily on a detailed study of the Classics, though Percival was a pioneer of Science education. There was, of course, no radio, no television and probably there was limited access even to books. Visiting lecturers addressed the School on a variety of topics and in the early years John Addington Symonds had enjoyed a special brief to enthrall the Sixth form with his enthusiasm for the Greek ideals: but these were infrequent experiences. Most lessons, one suspects, were rather a grind and there is no doubt that for most boys the pleasures of the Close and contests won and lost there lay at the forefront of their thinking. For those boys with awakening intellectual interests, it was probably a revelation, therefore, to be taken into the confidence of a few particular masters.

For Henry Newbolt, it was his housemaster, George Hyde Wollaston, who exercised the deepest and most lasting influence. Percival had appointed him in 1873 and two years later, when 'Town' boys were divided into two groups, Wollaston took charge of North Town, whose fortunes he guided all his time at Clifton. He chose never to be a boarding housemaster which would have been more remunerative and in some ways more prestigious. He lived with his family in an impressive house in College Road and was therefore a near neighbour of the Newbolts. The Wollastons lived stylishly, their drawing-room with its black carpet and elegant furnishings especially exciting admiration. He taught science and languages, but never to Newbolt in class; it was outside lesson time that he felt Wollaston's educational influence most. 'Every day and at all hours in his own rooms he was giving us a course in history, literature, internationalism and the art of travel. By his drawings, his familiarity with languages, customs and scenery, his specimens of odd minerals, we got to know of his habit of solitary tramping in foreign parts and his delight in their inhabitants; but it was chiefly the birds, beasts and butterflies which attracted him, and the physical aspect of the countries in which they lived.'[12] Mrs. Wollaston's role — like that of the first Mrs. Percival — should not be neglected. She 'was in complete contrast to him and therefore his perfect complement. She was as short as he was tall, as urbane as he was rugged, as pungently and audaciously witty as he was naïvely humorous. She was a Richmond, and had a full share of the gifts of that many-gifted family. For twenty years she was the nurse, mother, confidential aunt and smiling satirist of the North Town, and for the whole of that time and thirty years more she was admired and feared and quoted by all Clifton, town and College alike.'[13]

George Wollaston and his family were close friends of Newbolt for half a century and he never forgot the debt he owed him for the great gift of a liberal education. 'The rest I think I really might have got from books, or from any kind of teachers: but education he gave me perpetually'. When

Wollaston died in 1926 Newbolt wrote to a friend 'I can't tell you how his going empties the world — many other lights have gone, but it has never darkened more perceptibly than now. I had only one mother, and one Wollaston.'[14]

After his housemaster, Newbolt considered Sidney Irwin to be his greatest benefactor. Born in Australia of an English mother and Irish father, Irwin had studied at Wellington College and Oxford and taught for a time at Westminster School before arriving at Clifton in the same year as Newbolt. His greatest interests were Classical and English literature and in conversation on these subjects he was an inspiration. He loved Clifton, too, and had strong feelings about morals, manners, and loyalty. We ourselves are not important, was his message, but Clifton is and we derive *our* importance from serving her. It was he who later on successfully persuaded the school to adopt the motto '*Spiritus intus alit*', from a phrase taken from well-known lines of Virgil. According to J.M. Wilson, preaching in Clifton Chapel in 1913, what Virgil meant was 'a divine spirit giving life to the whole physical world: that is what those who chose this motto meant — a divine spirit giving life to the school and every member of it: and that is what every generation of us that live under this motto must understand and mean.'[15] Irwin's enthusiasm for loyalty to the institution was certainly not lost on Newbolt, in whom he undoubtedly found a kindred spirit. Long after Newbolt had moved out of his forms they would sit together of an evening reading the *Odyssey* 'for the mere pleasure of travel and companionship'. Towards the end of his career Irwin blossomed as a writer, contributing influential articles to *The Times Literary Supplement* and the *Quarterly Review* as well as publishing a biography of his friend and colleague T.E. Brown.

Brown was, of all assistant masters, the man who had the biggest reputation outside Clifton. He was a Manxman, born in Braddan, the son of the Vicar there. From King William's College he went on to a brilliant career at Oxford, followed by a return to his old school as Second Master and a brief tenure of the Headmastership of the King's School Gloucester. He was one of Percival's first appointments and he stayed at Clifton twenty years, Housemaster, Head of the 'Modern' side and Deputy Headmaster. He was perhaps a remote figure to the boys in his House, but his teaching and his conversation drew on resources of learning and experience widely recognised as unique. He lived a double life, partly the schoolmaster dominated by routine, partly the poet whose spirit roamed the Isle of Man even when his body was in Bristol —

I'm here at Clifton, grinding at the mill
My feet for thrice nine barren years have trod;
But there are rocks and waves at Scarlett still
And gorse runs riot in Glen Chass — thank God.[17]

Many of his poems were written in local dialect and he is remembered today as a major figure in Manx culture, a large room in the Douglas Museum being set aside to display his books, his furniture, his Clifton mortar-board. He did not teach Newbolt formally but again it was outside lesson-time that the work of education was most memorably done: 'I was now and then a guest at his table, and admired the broad full-flowing stream of his conversation —it was even fuller than his letters. His bodily presence matched it —he rolled into the room, the Close or the School Chapel like a deep flood on an incoming tide.'[18]

Brown was a working poet, and this must have impressed itself upon Newbolt, as upon many Cliftonians. Poetry at that time was held in high regard, even by schoolboys. After all, much of their time was spent reading works of the Classical poets: the ability to produce well-turned verses was much admired, and *The Cliftonian* magazine, appearing several times a term in those days, provided an opportunity for publication — and the standard was often high. To be a poet would certainly have seemed to the young Newbolt a noble calling.

'A remarkable, in some ways a unique, personality; one of the two or three best teachers of his time, an intellectual force of a high order and a moral prophet.'[19] Sir Herbert Warren, a former pupil, describes T.W. Dunn, another of the masters who impressed Newbolt. 'I fell completely under his spell and recognised in him a genuinely oracular personality. In school he taught me German, and that for only two hours in the week: but as he himself used to say, the lesson is nothing, the learning is all.'[20] A former Fellow of Peterhouse, Dunn had been enticed to Clifton by Percival — initially for one year, though he stayed ten, founding what is now called Wiseman's House before leaving Clifton on his appointment as first Headmaster of Bath College. Another boarding housemaster well known to Newbolt was E.M. Oakeley who befriended him at school and long afterwards: 'when he had retired to his beautiful island château on the Lake of Brienz, I used to visit him there and help him revise his Register and talk of old times and remember all the glories of our blood and state.'[21] Newbolt does not specifically mention Norman Moor, a brilliant classical scholar who returned to teach at his old school and was much loved by his pupils, or Graham Dakyns, the first of Percival's appointments, eccentric, original and a formative influence on the school: but they were there, part of the remarkable brotherhood of 'prophets' that guided Newbolt and the Cliftonians of his day.

Yet despite the undoubted intellectual stature of the staff and the eight or nine scholarships gained at the Universities in an average year it was not academic activity that lay at the very heart of Newbolt's Clifton. 'It is a mere truth to say that there were very few members of the school who would not have bartered away all chance of intellectual distinction for a place in the Cricket Eleven or Football Fifteen', he wrote.[22] As for art it was, according to his brother 'as far off as the Sahara and as little known . . . boys who had heard of Botticelli probably thought, like the young man in *Punch*, that it was a cheese. Cliftonians were Philistine to the last degree.'[23] The absolute devotion of the Public Schools to the games ideal between 1870 and 1914 is well known and well documented. In part it derived from the respect paid to the Classics, for in the pages of Greek and Latin authors the athlete glows as a heroic figure, as does the warrior. But for men like Percival games advanced the corporate life, promoting 'a growth of the sterner and more robust virtues — fortitude, self-reliance, intrepidity: devotion to the comon weal: readiness for united action and self-sacrifice. The value of our school life, in his view, was that it preserves and calls forth these same elements of character and recreates the old classic type.'[24] Moreover, Victorian headmasters were very much alive to the threat posed by sex in all its variable forms and vigorous participation in physical sports was thought likely not only to improve the physique but also to reduce the risks of moral decline. Percival drove those in his school to the point of exhaustion, a fact recorded by masters and boys alike.

All the evidence suggests that in his moral crusade Percival was remarkably successful both at Clifton and later at Rugby where it was necessary for him to restore the School's reputation. At Clifton, Quiller-Couch remembered, 'we were caught up in a cult of Roman stoicism and service suffused with Christianity; and some of us suffered. But this, too, resulted in some fine by-products, notably an Arnoldian consciousness of moral responsibility (too precocious perhaps) with a certain puritan scorn of defilement in conduct or speech. There could hardly have been, by instinct through habit, a *cleaner* school in England.' Its main characteristics, he thought, were 'freedom and curiosity of mind tempered by a severe conscience in all matters of service and duty, with a yet severer discouragement of any tendency in the individual to "side" or "swagger".'[25] Another who entered Clifton about 1870 later remembered how 'on the eve of my first coming here I met a sixth-form boy who had just left the school. As we talked, some little question of conduct came up for discussion. He made the remark "when you get to Clifton you will hear quite little boys characterise this or the other as bad form." What I found when I came, as the best gift of that former age, was the high moral atmosphere which we all breathed here. It insensibly toned and braced those who entered the school. I have said elsewhere and I have said truly that during the time I was here I knew of no morally unseemly deed done, and I heard no morally unseemly conversation. And that was the time when we proudly remembered that we have five Old Cliftonians in the Oxford Eleven and that when a football side was made up in the Parks Clifton used to play the rest'. This was the Dean of Gloucester, preaching at Commemoration in 1920. It is interesting that he went on to say 'I shall never forget the thrill with which I heard for the first time the lines by our Clifton poet which you know far too well for me to quote them, but I felt that at last someone had caught and put into poetry the very spirit of our corporate life here.'[26]

In fact Henry Newbolt was not a member of the School Cricket XI or the Football XV though during his time Clifton 'had an extraordinary succession of victories and our champions were almost as well known to the public as to ourselves . . . we went about our own work and play in a proud obscurity, content to know that we belonged to a great and famous fellowship'.[27] Other schools were not unaware of Clifton's preoccupation with sport. The school magazine's Editorial for July 1880 — about the time when Newbolt himself was editor — begins 'Some months ago our December number was severely criticised by some of our contemporaries for being for the most part devoted to nothing but accounts of football matches. Our contemporary would, doubtless, in like manner object to the decided predominance of cricket news in the present number; but it seems to us that when cricket is the only occupation in which any active and general interest is taken during the summer term, our pages will naturally be full — perhaps too full — of mere accounts of cricket matches.'[28] Sport was surrogate war, and a victory over a rival could provoke a massive outburst of loyalty from the boys of the school, thronging the streets to meet the returning heroes from the station, drawing their carriage in triumph or raising them shoulder high.[29] Though he never played for the XI — or perhaps because of this — the image of cricket as the supreme game was firmly implanted into Newbolt at Clifton, a seed that later flowered in the famous lines of *Vitaï Lampada*. Towards the end of his life he can still be found making use of the cricketing metaphor for literary purposes, this time to explain a common fault in sonnets. 'The first part is too often only the run up to the wicket; mechanical and not over-elegant, but followed by a really good ball which gets the middle stump.'[30]

Yet it was not so much in team games as in contests requiring individual skills that Newbolt prospered most. From the start Clifton laid great emphasis on cross-country running and the curiously named Short and Long Penpole races were the highlight of each Easter term. Newbolt had the spare, athletic frame of a good runner and later recalled cross-country rivalry in a poem addressed to his contemporary F.E. Younghusband —

Do you remember when the Downs were white
With the March dust from highways glaring bright,
How you and I, like yachts that toss the foam,
From Penpole Fields came stride and stride for home?
One grimly leading, one intent to pass,
Mile after mile we measured road and grass,
Twin silent shadows, till the hour was done,
The shadows parted and the stouter won.[31]

A fascination for history, heraldry, chivalry and the role of the warrior, together with the persuasiveness of the Commanding Officer, Colonel Plant, led Newbolt to forsake the Close and the pleasures of cricket for the less glamorous though still rewarding activities of the Cadet Corps and the Bedminster rifle range. He did not enjoy the drill and missed the cricket and the sacrificed half-holidays, but he rose to be Captain of the School Corps as well as the Shooting VIII. As a marksman he won the Regimental Challenge Cup for Officers in 1880 and shot in two successive years in the inter-school competitions on Wimbledon Common. 'There was another kind of "corporate life": there — apart from the Shields and Cups and bi-diurnal Prizes for which we could shoot all day long — we found a new and friendly fellowship in which a hundred schools were represented.'[32] It was to be, despite all his writing about warfare and warriors, his only spell in uniform.

So there is substance in the high claims made for Clifton by those who studied there in the 1870s and 1880s. The school was ruled by a great Headmaster and served by teachers of distinction: it was vigorous, healthy, successful in academic work and games. Such a place was bound to make a deep impression upon those whose most formative years were spent there. They certainly left Clifton feeling they had a positive duty to do their best both for their school and in a wider sense their country and many did not disappoint. O.F. Christie in *Clifton School Days*, published in 1930, carried out some research on what became of the boys in the Sixth Form during his first year in the school, 1879, and in his last year, 1885.[33] Both lists are impressive and as the first consists of Newbolt's contemporaries, it is worth reciting the names —

Upper Bench

Sir Thomas Heath, F.R.S.	Joint Permanent Secretary to the Treasury
Christopher Cookson	Fellow of Magdalen College Oxford
Rev. Arthur St. John Gray	Headmaster of Malvern College
George C. Harrison	Oxford double first and Cricket blue Clifton master
Spencer Nash	Scholar of Balliol. 1st class in Mods.
Herbert Turner	F.R.S. Savilian Professor of Astronomy at Oxford
Lewis Fry	1st class Mods., New College. Artist
Henry Cooper	Headmaster, Lichfield Grammar School
George Dance	Indian Civil Service
John Bradshaw	Clifton Master
Rev. Westley Bothamley	Anglican parson

Lower Bench

Sir Henry Newbolt	C.H. Poet, Journalist, Man of letters
George Heaton	1st class Nat. Science at Oxford. Lecturer, Birmingham University
Arthur Jose	*The Times* correspondent in Australia. Editor, *Encyclopaedia of Australia*
Hugh Cookson	Indian Civil Service
Arthur Baker	Professor of Philosophy at the Independent College, Taunton
Thomas Wilson	Indian Civil Service
Francis Reynolds	'A great all-round athlete'
Henry Heath	Major General, C.B.
Sir Alexander Pinhey	Resident, Hyderabad
Clement Kent	Author
Rev. Reginald Talbot	D.D. Canon of Bristol, Archdeacon of Swindon
Edwin Cannan	Professor of Political Economy, London University
John Clarke	Professor of Medicine at Bristol University
Sir Richard Threlfall	K.B.E., F.R.S. Professor of Physics, University of Sydney

If it seems odd that there should have been a Sixth Form of only 26 boys in a school of nearly 700 it must be remembered that the examination structure then was very different from today. The 'Sixth', as at Arnold's Rugby, contained the intellectual élite, those who would be groomed for University distinctions: meanwhile, with their canes as wands of office, they helped to discipline the younger boys and entered into a more privileged relationship with their masters.

Newbolt later lamented that a high proportion of his intimate school friends had died prematurely: 'Will Threlfall and Reggie Wood were drowned in early days: Hugh Cookson died of typhoid in India, Lyon was scalped by Indians in Arizona, the three Hobart-Hampdens, our close neighbours and daily companions, are all gone.'[34] However, as his ties with Clifton remained very close for the rest of his life, he came to know well many whom he had seldom spoken to at school. One of these was Douglas Haig, a School House boy. 'I chanced to sit next to him for one term in Big Side Levée — the games committee — and was interested and amused by his short, dry remarks, uttered in a Scots accent that made them, for me who had never been in Scotland, much more difficult to translate than any Latin. But what really captivated me was the fine figure he made in the Close, with his powerful stature and handsome face. He had from the first that striking combination of resolute chin, clear eyes and placid brow — a face not easy to read, but impossible to mistrust or belittle. I believe that in an unofficial biography — not by a Cliftonian — he is described as having been obscure at school. This does not tally with my recollection. Haig was never high in the school lists — he left early for Oxford and Sandhurst — but he was already a marked man.'[35] The Clifton connection brought Haig and Newbolt together a good deal in after years: Haig, a man to whom words did not come easily, admired the poet: Newbolt, never quite a man of action, envied the paladin. Both were archetypes of Percival's Clifton.

Newbolt wrote poems at school, mostly lyrics and epigrams, the latter sometimes composed during Irwin's lessons while the master's attention was elsewhere. Some pieces of his work were printed in *The Cliftonian* magazine but they were 'signed with deceptive initials' and were with one exception printed after he had left for Oxford. Certainly the 1881 and 1882 editions of the magazine contain a number of poems with a Newboltian ring to them but their author never felt subsequently that they were worth rescuing from anonymity and they lie there still, subjects for a guessing game. The trouble was that Newbolt had a rival, a Cornish lad who had won a scholarship into the Sixth Form — and Dakyns' House — where on his first day he took against his new housemaster for criticising his study curtains. This was Arthur Quiller-Couch whose poem *Athens* (eight pages long) Newbolt had good cause to remember.[36] 'We had, of course an Annual School Prize for English Verse and (T.E.) Brown was the judge who awarded it — at any rate in my last year, when I entered for it, with a hundred and twenty lines of blank verse. I had no hope of success: Couch was my only competitor, but I knew that he would do something far more attractive than my hectic piece, and so he did. When Brown came across me the next day he said, with humour in his eye. "I'm sorry I couldn't give you the English Verse: but you see . . . there was Couch." '[37]

Another contemporary with whom Newbolt maintained a lifelong friendship was Rowland Whitehead. His father Sir James had, like John Percival, been a pupil at Appleby Grammar School and, rising to be Lord Mayor of London and a wealthy man, he was a generous benefactor of Clifton, as was his son. Rowland Whitehead was the first Secretary of the O.C. Society and in 1898 he made a speech at the Commemoration Supper in which he described the three main virtues of Clifton as he perceived them. 'The first', he said, 'was strenuousness, a strenuousness which pervaded every department of school life. I fancy that the most withering term of contempt in our vocabulary was the word "loafer" or "slacker". The second feature was a certain robustness of tone, a manliness, using that term . . . as involving a hatred of luxury, a contempt for self-indulgence . . . and a love in the main of simplicity and naturalness and even severity of taste. The third feature . . . was our devotion to the common weal, our patriotism, as we boldly called it: an exalted standard of public spirit and a willingness to surrender personal aims in the football field or the cricket field for the sake of the common good.'[38]

Not that every boy was inflamed with this particular spirit. One who arrived at Clifton the year Newbolt left was the young Roger Fry 'a weedy boy with retreating chin and spectacles hiding the bright large eyes.' Despite outward conformity he resented 'the whole Public School system, and all those Imperialistic and patriotic emotions which it enshrined.'[39] Eventually he found a sympathiser, a boy described by Fry's sister as having an ill-fixed head and inordinate length of body, 'like a greatly elongated tadpole'.[40] This was John Ellis McTaggart, recognised even at Clifton as a genius, later a famous philosopher and a friend of Newbolt.

It is possible to claim that there were at Clifton at about the same time as Newbolt a number of boys who subsequently became dominating influences in their chosen fields. There was Haig the soldier; Sir Charles

Firth the historian of 17th century England; Quiller-Couch the literary critic; McTaggart the philosopher; J.H. Whitley, Speaker of the House of Commons; Harry Plunket Greene the tenor whose name became synonymous with the drawing room ballad; Roger Fry the art critic ('in so far as taste can be changed by one man', wrote Kenneth Clark, 'it was changed by Roger Fry'), and Newbolt himself. Through these men of vigour and originality, as well as others, the influence of Percival's Clifton made itself felt way beyond the boundaries of the College Close.

It was Percival's Clifton, yet he was not the only Headmaster most of these boys knew. Percival left at the end of the Easter term 1879, when Newbolt still had two years of school ahead of him. He could not stay for ever; back in 1874 he had been a candidate for the Headmastership of Rugby, to the consternation of Clifton. When it was learnt that he would not after all be going a subscription was raised to complete the north range of the Percival Library as a thank-offering. But in 1878 he accepted the Presidency of Trinity College, Oxford, which rather shocked opinion in the University as he was not a Trinity man and he was known to be a Liberal. It was not quite a poisoned chalice, but he knew it would not be easy. He felt he could leave Clifton because James Wilson had agreed to succeed him. There were, of course, emotional scenes of valediction, a farewell sermon, presentations and a dinner followed by twelve speeches, dutifully reported in 28 pages of *The Cliftonian*.[41] On the last day of term it was the custom for the Headmaster to read the Lists and for the senior member of the Sixth Form present to call for three cheers. As it happened that particular honour fell to Henry Newbolt. Dr. Percival 'mounted the stone staircase as far as the first landing, turned to look down upon us, and removed his trencher cap. Then, as if from a statue, we heard a clear, emotionless voice, without haste, without rest, reading out an unending sequence of names. At last came a moment of silence — it was broken by a word of command shouted in a hard staccato voice — "Three cheers for the Headmaster!" I heard the words with no realisation that I had uttered them myself.'[42] So Percival was gone: but not really. He became a member of the College Council the year after he left and was Chairman from 1895 until 1917, the year before he died. He was buried below the high altar of Clifton Chapel, and his body lies there still.

Though he shared Percival's dedication to Clifton, Liberal religious views and wide-ranging social concern, the Rev. James Maurice Wilson was in most other respects a complete contrast to his predecessor. 'If Percival had any human weaknesses', Newbolt wrote 'we never saw them. Wilson had no classic outlines, he was human to the core and betrayed it in every tone and gesture — his emotional nature was aptly symbolised by his flowing beard, and at any moment of intense feeling, serious or humorous, his voice would crack suddenly with heart-shaking effect. His intellect was scientific but his nature was Franciscan and pastoral'.[43] Wilson was born in 1836 one of twins, on the Isle of Man at King William's College where his father was the first Principal. Later he went to school there and met for the first time a senior boy called T.E. Brown. An awakening interest in mathematics led him to move to the Grammar School at Sedbergh where that subject was taught seriously. He moved to St. John's College at Cambridge where careful coaching and an average of seven hours' work a day won Wilson the position of Senior Wrangler: but soon after the examination he had a nervous breakdown, emerging from convalescence with his mind almost a blank in mathematical matters except for algebra and Euclid. This did not prevent his election as a Fellow of St. John's and his appointment as science master at Rugby School: in fact he had not studied science at Cambridge and chiefly taught mathematics, at that time regarded as very much a downgrade study compared with the Classics. At Rugby he strove to advance the prestige of his subject and his controversial book emphasising the unsuitability of Euclid as a textbook for schools made him a prominent figure in mathematics circles.[44]

Wilson knew Percival well as the young man who had joined the Rugby staff the year after his own appointment and a strong mutual respect had been established between the two. His wife's recent death had caused a domestic crisis which had led to thoughts of giving up schoolmastering, but Wilson was the man Percival wanted to succeed him. It was a wise choice. Wilson was popular from the first and during his twelve years Clifton continued to develop and expand.

Newbolt came to know Wilson more intimately than he could have hoped to have known Percival. The proximity of the Newbolt household to School House was certainly an advantage here for College masters were often entertained by Mrs. Newbolt in Worcester Crescent. Newbolt's father had married his first wife in Kirk Braddan, on the Isle of Man, and when Wilson discovered this at the Newbolts' house one evening, he suggested that Henry should accompany him when he visited his own relations in Douglas during the Easter holidays. This excursion gave Newbolt a privileged opportunity to observe his Headmaster off duty, not least as he recited T.E. Brown's dialect poem *Betsy Lee* during the four hour sea crossing from Liverpool. Once arrived, 'our stay in the island was a faithful pilgrimage to all places sacred to Brown's genius. We tramped to the house where he was born and to the glens and coves and villages named

1 The Rev. Henry Francis Newbolt, 1824–1866.

2 Emily Newbolt (née Stubbs), 1838–1921.

3 Henry John Newbolt, aged twelve.

4 Francis George Newbolt, aged eleven.

in his poems: we believed that we were getting to understand him better both as a man and as a poet, for our re-examination of him in his native setting. This was not all I learnt in our wanderings. Wilson had little or no self-consciousness — he gave away all his thoughts and tastes and personal characteristics with careless generosity, even to a boy one third his own age'.[45] The point was, doubtless, that Wilson recognised in Newbolt rather a remarkable boy.

Editor of *The Cliftonian*, Captain of the Shooting VIII, Captain of the Corps, Head of North Town, Head of School for the Easter term in the absence of Spencer Nash, Newbolt in his last year had every opportunity of showing himself to be the public spirited servant of the community that it was Clifton's purpose to produce. We may assume that he carried out his duties meticulously, that he maintained high standards, that he handled his juniors sensitively, though with reserve. Above all he was conscientious and he played the man: in a reflective moment in 1916 he wrote 'I myself was a good deal older at nineteen than I have ever been since'.[46] In December 1880 he tried for a Balliol scholarship with three of his contemporaries in the Sixth; Nash, Jose and Boas. They enjoyed their week in Oxford and all were successful except Newbolt. Norman Moor, who had taught him, made enquiries and discovered that some examiners had found fault with an essay he had written on 'Biography'. Failure at Balliol was certainly a disappointment, possibly a humiliation, but he sat the examination for Corpus Christi College in a snowbound January 'all the better for the Arctic silence and seclusion in which we dealt with our papers'. This time he won a scholarship and could return to Clifton to concentrate on his strenuous duties as acting Head of School. The end of a school career, certainly one as successful as Newbolt's, is sometimes attended by emotion and nostalgia, but again, being a dayboy made all the difference: 'I had no feeling, even when the last day of term came, that I was leaving Clifton — I was a domiciled Cliftonian, not a boarder, and the school, with all its resources, would still be within easy reach of my home.'[47]

August of that year was spent in Switzerland with his family. Mrs. Newbolt had not been abroad before and this excursion was a compliment to her grown-up son who led the party. Henry and Frank were fascinated by unfamiliar Swiss ways and defended them stoutly against their mother's views that foreign children were generally to be pitied for having 'to live abroad all their lives'.[48] September must have presented Newbolt with a new and strange experience: the great buildings of Clifton College, readily visible from the windows of Worcester Crescent, were all at once roused from their summer quietude by the invasion of over 600 boys ready for the excitements of a new school year. Frank joined them of course but not his elder brother who had to wait — perhaps impatiently — for October, and Oxford.

PART THREE: 1881–1885

'The City is a fairy city, neither in the world nor of it'

Corpus Christi has charm and atmosphere in full measure, but it is not one of Oxford's grander colleges. Newbolt's sacred sense of loyalty forbade any slighting comparisons but one so sensitive to the spectacle of the Close at Clifton cannot at first have been unconscious of the splendours of Christ Church and Merton, the grandiose neighbours of his own College. Bishop Fox of Winchester had founded Corpus in the reign of Henry VIII and endowed it with a fine Quadrangle, Hall, Chapel and Library: it had flourished as a place of learning and reared many famous sons, most recently John Keble and Thomas Arnold. In the 1870's and 1880's Corpus admitted five or six Scholars and about twelve Commoners each year, so the undergraduates would not have numbered much more than seventy. It should be remembered that Newbolt had not lived away from home for several years and neither his rooms nor the College servants, if the account in *The Twymans* is to be believed, impressed him favourably at first. His rooms 'adjoined the tower over the entrance-gate of the College, up two flights of a turning staircase, and looked out on to one side of Oriel across a narrow street. The bedroom was cramped and uncarpeted; the sitting-room, though well proportioned, had a very low ceiling, and looked dark on so gloomy a day as this. Percival turned in dismay to the under-porter, who was conducting him —

"Is there no choice of rooms?"

"Oh, yes, sir," the man replied, with an odious tone of managing servility. The best rooms are always reserved for the scholars, sir. Mr. Marjoribanks had the first choice; I think you were second scholar, sir, and this is the second best set — the second best for gentlemen of your year, sir."

Then as Percival remained silent, he added, "This is the Founder's Tower, sir, a very quiet staircase — there's only the Dean and one senior gentleman below you, sir."

A quick, heavy foot was heard on the stairs; the under-porter vanished suddenly and his place was taken by a black thick-set man who informed Percival in a tone of absolute mastery that he was his servant.'[2] Anyone familiar with that splendid functionary the Oxford 'scout' will know exactly what Newbolt meant. For his second and third years, however, he moved to the Fellows' buildings and rooms that had been occupied by Ruskin, no less, during his time as Slade Professor. There was not only the Professor's sitting-room carpet but also Parisian wallpapers specially chosen by Ruskin to decorate the bedroom and ante-room. But more than that, there was a view across one of Oxford's greatest glories, Christ Church Meadow: it surpassed even Clifton's Close. 'I had never anywhere at any time been at home in a scene of such ancient peace and beauty. It gave me again and again the pure luxury of a trance — it carried me out of the natural existence of thought and activity into a region of more convincing reality, where intensity of feeling and imagination took the place of Time. That might be on a summer night, when all windows were open and not a sound to be heard but the *crake-crake* of a bird down in Christ Church meadows: or on a warm spring morning when the sun poured a flood of light across my room, in which motes danced and smoke — wreaths whirled and widened and dispersed, while the Self sat in the centre of a boundless solitude and enjoyed an Everlasting Now.'[3]

John Percival's Clifton had emphasised the virtues of scholarship, sporting prowess and 'high tone' and Newbolt's Oxford career pursued a course that would not have displeased the Great Man — fortunately, perhaps, for as President of Trinity College Percival was a major figure in Oxford and doubtless kept a wary eye open for Cliftonians. Newbolt and his mother called on him almost as soon as they arrived in Oxford. Mrs. Newbolt informed the President that they had just seen the aged Cardinal Newman in what she described as Trinity's 'front yard'. It was Percival the builder of quadrangles who replied: 'Yes,' he said, 'there has been perhaps some neglect in the past: but we may be making improvements presently.'[4] Percival was at Oxford during the whole of Newbolt's undergraduate career and it must be assumed that his close proximity to one who had in any case been a devoted admirer served only to strengthen the spell that Clifton had cast over him. One evening, for instance, he attended a dance in the Common Room at All Souls. 'This made a ballroom of an uncommon sort — the smooth floor was like a mirror and the dark panelled walls were festooned with brilliant half-circles of wax candles in shining glasses. In this scene — set apparently for some comedy of the eighteenth century — I saw as in a queer dream Dr. Percival looking on with his marmoreal smile fixed in enigmatic curves while I danced — yes danced — before his eyes — with his daughter Bessie, a child friend of old Clifton days. It was a pleasant dream, but with a shiver of apprehension blowing through it — was the Censor of my youth smiling sincerely, or was he secretly "not amused" by our giddy revolutions?'[5]

The Honours course in Classics at Oxford spanned four years with an examination chiefly in linguistic skills after two years (Moderations) and a final examination called 'Literae Humaniores' (Greats). Newbolt's tutor for the first part of the course was a man who represented yet another link with Clifton. This was Arthur Sidgwick, the brother-in-law of James Wilson. By now in his early forties he had, before taking up his Fellowship at Corpus, served as a master at Rugby for fifteen years. He made contact with Newbolt on his first day in College and took him off to a meeting of the Browning Society where his paper on the poet's love poems made a profound impression on the young undergraduate. The occasion is recalled in detail not only in his memoirs, but in *The Twymans* —

' "Who is this Mr. Hedgeley?" Althea asked Percy as she sipped the tea which he had hastened to offer her.

"The Hedger?" he replied. "He was my Mods. tutor — the best in Oxford. It is a splendid piece of luck that he should be reading when you are here — there's no one near him for things of this sort . . ."

Althea marked Mr. Hedgeley at once: a handsome man with a fine forehead, and a blush-rose complexion which combined rather oddly with his flowing beard of silver. He seemed to be amusing those who stood near him with a series of delicately dramatic stories. "What a nice quick way he has" she said — "that way of laughing heartily and getting it over and going on again. Yes, I think there is something different about him."

Percy's criticism was generally light enough, but he was always serious when he praised a friend. "I assure you", he said gravely, "that he is the man in all Oxford who has made the most difference to me." '[6]

Guided by Sidgwick, Newbolt experienced few difficulties with the course for Mods. and, in common with many who were Scholars, sat for the examination in his fourth, rather than his sixth term. His own comment on the academic standards of school and university is revealing: 'Moderations were of course important as the final test of Classical Scholarship, and a First Class was a necessity for any man who wished to enter the teaching profession with an undeniable certificate. But two years was far too much to spend on it — the Public School standard was now so high that any man who had secured a good College Scholarship could probably have taken a First in Mods. very shortly afterwards. The only really new ground to be covered was Logic, and a few books hitherto unread, such as Lucretius and Theocritus. These three subjects were the only ones on which I can remember spending much time, and the work was more of a pleasure than an effort'.[7] He took some reading on his summer vacation climbing party in Switzerland and returned to sit the exam in the Michaelmas term. It was a good year for Corpus: six firsts, with Newbolt among them. No wonder that 'the Christmas vacation went merrily in a round of congratulations.'[8]

Three summers later Newbolt had to come to terms with his 'second' in 'Greats', which he described as 'more than a disappointment, a catastrophe . . . it was a blow to self-confidence and had a bewildering effect.'[9] When the news arrived by telegram he was at the house of friends whose own son had also gained a second and regarded it as a cause for celebration, so Newbolt affected to make light of the affair. But there can be no doubt that for him this result was a major disappointment. Clifton had trained him to reach only for the topmost branches of the tree. By way of explanation Newbolt suggests in his autobiography that his tutors for the 'Greats' course at Oxford had encouraged him to develop wider interests: his tutor Tommy Case, for instance, had advocated the merits of English Literature while the President of Corpus, T.H. Fowler, was keen to see Newbolt immersed in the social round. So there was much general reading, much argument with his contemporaries, debating at the Oxford Union where he stood (unsuccessfully) for Librarian, dances in his College rooms and house parties in the vicinity of Oxford. The University was very much a male preserve, as Clifton had been, but this did not mean that feminine influence was entirely excluded.

The first romantic affair that we are told about took place in Newbolt's last year at Clifton where he developed an attachment for one of his sister's school friends. Disaster, as Newbolt thought, overcame them one evening when his Housemaster viewed them kissing in the shadows. Nervous about the expected rebuke Newbolt spent a few anxious days before receiving from Wollaston a copy of *Vita Nuova* inscribed by the donor, 'Good is the Lordship of Love, for that it draws away the mind of his servant from all things mean.'[10] The reader will search in vain throughout the works or the life of Newbolt for explicit sexual references. Love for him was a romantic ideal tinged, perhaps, with duty: relationships with women involved courtesy, consideration and good taste. Yet he needed the company of women and several were to be vitally important influences in his life. It was at Oxford, prompted by Browning's poetry, that Newbolt's admiration for the 'idyllic and transient' style of Tennysonian love declined in favour of a more full-blooded concept. 'To the lovers of to-day', Newbolt observed, 'all this will probably appear very ordinary doctrine — directly or indirectly the Browning lesson has been learned — and I think understood. But to a lover nineteen years of age in 1881 it was a great enlightenment . . .'.[11]

So there were young ladies to captivate him, often the daughters of dons with whom he established special friendships — Max Müller, for example, with whose family 'I must have spent more hours in my last year than with any other friends in Oxford'.[12] Then there was the daughter of Professor Legge who had 'a spell beyond explanation — she might any day have anticipated Max Beerbohm's enchantress Zuleika Dobson, for whose sake the men of a whole College drowned themselves in the Isis on the same afternoon.'[13] Newbolt himself was not negligent in paying homage to the river, which in these years lay at the very centre of Oxford life. The success of the University Eight in its annual tryst with Cambridge and of the College eight in the bumping races was much to be desired. Newbolt had noted that after Clifton it came as a disappointment to know that 'Games had not the same militant edge to them: College played College at football, cricket or tennis — we desired that Corpus should win, but how much did it matter if we lost to Balliol, where we had so many friends . . .'[14] Rowing alone excited the patriotic loyalty of the entire University. Newbolt would have been proud of the fact that in 1881 the young god standing, as President of the University Boat Club, at the very pinnacle of athletic renown was an Old Cliftonian, Richard Kindersley.[15] To be an oarsman was more or less compulsory for a man of suitable physique and there is every reason to suppose that Newbolt would have sought glory on the river but for his slight stature. Unfortunately at nine and a half stone he was too light for an oarsman and too heavy for a cox. So he did not row and his main university interests were intellectual rather than sporting. But on the river loyalty was involved, and evoked a warm response. Loyalty was to be a main theme in Newbolt's life and writing, and he practised what he preached. 'I have never been able to agree with H.G. Wells who once wrote to me reproaching me for wasting time on "these petty loyalties". Loyalty is a quality, not a quantity, and cannot be petty: nor is the obligation to practise it any less binding in smaller affairs than in greater.'[16] He cheered the College Eight with the best of them, and rejoiced when Corpus rowed Head of the River in his last term. As for the Boat Race, his brother Francis, still at school, recalls that in March 1883 'The "Bard of Avon Society" held its first meeting, at our house, and read part of *Henry IV* . . . At the second meeting we had a distinguished visitor, to wit my brother, the great Undergraduate, and he was in good spirits, as Oxford had won the Boat Race earlier in the day by three clear lengths.'[17]

All these worthy recreations, together with the fact that his tutor Tommy Case was unable through illness to act as one of the examiners for Greats and was replaced by 'the very Professor whose lecture he had been told to disregard' doubtless took their toll when examination time came round. Yet there were no firsts in Greats at Corpus that year, which led Newbolt to think in terms of tutorial mismanagement. When he taxed Case with this the reply came back that 'what he was sure of was that we had all had a real education — a thing which could not be expressed by marks.'[18] Years later a letter reached Newbolt informing him that he had been elected to an honorary Fellowship at Corpus. It was signed by the President of the College, Tommy Case.

It had not, in the strictest sense, been a University career of great distinction. No brilliant examination results with a Fellowship to follow; no University prizes; no Presidency of the Union; no athletic laurels. Instead he had done what the vast majority of Oxford undergraduates achieve, namely spent several very enjoyable years in a place of great beauty, extending his social and intellectual horizons. 'I had hoped and believed that Oxford would be a second Clifton, with every kind of opportunity and contest and pleasure magnified in value',[19] he wrote later. In fact he found the University much less strenuous, less competitive, less demanding of loyalty. This probably disappointed him, though he warmed to Oxford's image describing it, in *The Twymans*, as well as anyone can in a few words. 'The real charm of Oxford and the life men live there is not be seen or imagined from outside. It is not an effect of mere sentiment, aroused by the presence of beautiful buildings, of immemorial customs, of gardens laid with ancient turf and shadowed by stately trees. It does not lie in the quality of learning that is offered there, or the pastimes and pleasures that abound in many kinds: nor in the prestige of the great names of the past, nor the morning freshness of youth. To all these there is one thing added: the city is a fairy city, neither in the world nor of it, neither far from the world nor oblivious of it; it stands solitary but near by, as it were upon the cloud-hills of dawn, at the meeting-place of all yesterdays and all to-morrows, and its life is timeless.'[20]

PART FOUR: 1885–1898

'Am I just a ballad-monger who loves the sea and seamen?'

Newbolt came down from Oxford just in time to attend the Commemoration celebrations at Clifton, and shortly afterwards James Wilson pressed him to accept a teaching appointment at the College, while Percival offered to secure for him a tutorship at Oxford. He would certainly have been a most punctilious teacher while his acute administrative skills and strong sense of responsibility would have marked him out for rapid promotion, certainly in a school. He later wrote that what he was always looking for was 'the sense of a corporate life' and it is in some ways surprising that he did not leap at the chance to join Wilson's staff. In fact he had already decided to read for the Bar, perhaps because despite his undoubted scholarly interests and intellectual tastes he was to be at heart a man of affairs, keen to make some sort of impression upon the wider world. He was very sociable, he made friends easily, his company and conversation was welcome to men and women of distinction. His autobiography, especially when dealing with the years after Oxford, is full of the famous people he met and the many country houses he visited, though it is all related far too naturally for mere social-climbing to be suspected. In the world of elegance and intellectual wisdom he found his rightful and undisputed place.

In the autumn of 1885 he took rooms in London and found the work at Lincoln's Inn congenial to begin with. Leisure hours were spent meeting such figures as Oscar Wilde at smart parties, or seeing *The Mikado* at the Savoy Theatre or, by contrast, helping out at boys' clubs in Bethnal Green and Notting Hill where it seems that he developed a healthy respect for the sturdy independence of working-class lads: 'they were intelligible, admirable and lovable human beings, and I felt, as Percival would have said, that our life, on both sides, had become a different thing by the mere fact of our coming together. Certainly they enlarged my idea of patriotism.'[2] Percival had strongly supported the idea of 'mission' work in the industrial City, and here Newbolt was surely following his example.

He qualified as a barrister in the summer of 1887, the year of Queen

Victoria's Golden Jubilee. Yet as a bachelor he felt rather lost in London, and had persuaded his mother to move the family house from Clifton to a villa near Weybridge from which he could commute to his work. He had become accustomed to the role of head of the household but as his brother and sister grew up, his authority slipped away. Frank had become a legendary cricketer at Clifton as well as Captain of the Cadet Corps. A strapping six foot three he had gone up to Balliol where he captained the Eleven and was befriended by the formidable Dr. Jowett. Soon he, too, was to read for the Bar, to marry a daughter of the Master of University College and embark upon a successful career leading to knighthood and distinction as a lawyer. Even little Milly had blossomed into a charming young lady and was soon snapped up by one of Newbolt's legal colleagues, Thomas Chitty. By the end of 1888 Henry was the only unmarried Newbolt.

It did not last long. In his undergraduate days he had been taken up by the Chilton family who had a house in Surrey and a villa at Lynton on the North Devon coast. Newbolt had enjoyed a number of adventures with the Chiltons and their circle, including an excursion in the summer of 1887 when a train had been hired to convey the family party to Lynton. It stopped at Yeovil station where a self-possessed young lady 'in a straw hat with a lilac satin ribbon, and with a basket of purple grapes on her arm' stepped aboard. This was Miss Margaret Duckworth, daughter of the Squire of Orchardleigh in Somerset, and Newbolt was captivated at once by her cool serenity and classical good looks. Also 'she was a good musician, a first-rate walker, and very ready to fall in with our energetic way of life. We sang, of course: we watched the staghounds, we chased the fox, we caught trout and trawled for prawns, we climbed "through the Gull Rock," . . . we drove or tramped to every Hill of Vision on Exmoor,' and by the end of a fortnight Newbolt had firmly decided to marry her.[3]

He lost no time in announcing his plans to his hosts, and through them, to Margaret's parents. He returned to Clifton to plan his strategy, seeking advice from Wollaston and James Wilson who 'received me with shouts of laughter — a letter had already come from Mr. Duckworth asking for information about my character and prospects'.[4] All the signs were promising: the parental generation was not opposed to the match but the one person not yet consulted was Margaret herself who decided that she was not going to be hurried into marriage in this way. So Newbolt had to wait a whole year during which he courted the lady with all the chivalry and charm of the medieval heroes he was later to describe in his books. His reward came the next summer during another holiday in Lynton; at an early morning hour they became engaged amid the suitably romantic scenery of the Valley of the Rocks. The marriage took place in August 1889 in the thirteenth century church standing by a lake in the Park at Orchardleigh, the Duckworth's ancient house. No setting could have been more appropriate for Newbolt: here, at the heart of a landed estate, wedded to his lady in a church six hundred years old, he was marrying Time itself.

They moved into a small house in London, No.14 Victoria Road, W., which harboured them for eight years and saw the birth of two children and Newbolt's first books. It was not that he had really intended to be a writer, but he gradually slipped into the habit. His gift for mastering detail commended him to the task of writing anonymously a Law Digest, codifying legal decisions. This was a formidable task: there were 20,000 entries under the title 'Will' alone. But increasingly he found conveyancing tedious and does not really seem to have put his heart and soul into the work of a barrister. He was soon preferring to spend Thursday afternoons in the company of his wife and two of her literary friends, her cousin Ella Coltman and Mary Coleridge, a great-niece of the poet.

It was in this domestic circle that Newbolt's first literary work took shape, for each member of the quartet composed poems and stories and read them aloud. One of these stories found favour with the publishers Chatto and Windus and appeared in 1892 under the title *Taken from the Enemy*. It is a yarn of some 170 pages, set in 1821 and telling the story of an adventurous plan to rescue the Emperor Napoleon from his exile on St. Helena by means of a submarine. Napoleon unfortunately dies, thus thwarting the scheme. It is a tale told rather in the manner of *Treasure Island*, and Newbolt sent a copy to Robert Louis Stevenson who wrote back to say 'I took up your story after dinner and finished it before I slept, with a real amusement . . . Your plot is ingenious, particularly in the end.'[5] It still reads perfectly well today, making no great demands on the intellect. There are however one or two unmistakeably Newboltian passages, pointing the future way — as when the hero (Dick) reflects that 'Not only had he given his word to her . . . but duty called upon him now with a claim no less binding than that of loyalty to his promise.'[6] And as his ship sailed past Cape Trafalgar Dick 'felt his breath quicken with a great inspiration and his hands clench with the fighting instinct of his race.'[7]

Newbolt's second published venture, *Mordred*, was not so well received. A five-act drama in blank verse, it seeks to portray King Arthur more in

41

the original spirit of Malory's sinner than of Tennyson's hero. Some critics complained that Newbolt's verse did not stand comparison with that of the Laureate: others felt that blank verse was not the best medium for a play. It was printed in one limited edition in 1895 and copies today are rare. There is one in the library of Corpus Christi College, but the hardness of Bishop Fox's Tudor benches combines with the dullness of Newbolt in a blank verse mood to render the work more or less unreadable. Writing poetry was not, of course, a new venture for him. We have seen how he vied with Quiller-Couch at Clifton, leaving some of his verses 'buried in the School Magazine.' The first of his poems to gain a wide public was *Admirals All* which appeared in *Longman's Magazine* in 1895.

> Effingham, Grenville, Raleigh, Drake,
>   Here's to the bold and free!
> Benbow, Collingwood, Byron, Blake,
>   Hail to the Kings of the Sea!
> Admirals all, for England's sake,
>   Honour be yours and fame!
> And honour, as long as waves shall break,
>   To Nelson's peerless name!

Early in the following year a famous international incident occurred to provide a remarkably appropriate background for the publication of one of Newbolt's best poems, *Drake's Drum*.

On January 3rd 1896 the Emperor of Germany cabled to President Kruger of the Transvaal republic in South Africa which had just beaten off a small invasion force led by the celebrated Dr. Jameson and apparently inspired by the British Government: 'I sincerely congratulate you that, without appealing for the help of friendly Powers, you with your people, by your own energy against the armed hordes which as disturbers of the peace broke into your country, have succeeded in re-establishing peace and maintaining the independence of your country against attacks from without.'[8] The British public, already stung by constant French opposition as well as an unexpected row with the United States, had hoped that Queen Victoria's grandson could be relied on for support. The 'Kruger telegram' provoked an outbreak of spontaneous fury in Britain. The navy was called upon to send to sea a powerful flying squadron capable of crushing any opposition. As it happened the flagship of this force was named *Revenge* and a certain Captain Drake was the Commander of the marines aboard her.

Drake he's in his hammock an' a thousand mile away,
    (Capten, art tha sleepin' there below?),
Slung atween the round shot in Nombre Dios Bay,
    An' dreamin' arl the time o' Plymouth Hoe. . . .

Drake's Drum appeared in the *St. James's Gazette* on 15th January. The next day's news was that the Flying Squadron had put to sea. 'You'll never write anything better than that' the poet Robert Bridges told Newbolt. 'It isn't given to man to write anything better than that. I wish I had ever written anything half so good'.[9]

Though he had no reason to suspect it, Newbolt was very soon to become famous. He had visited Robert Bridges several times at his home in Yattendon, taking with him several manuscript poems. Bridges was impressed and passed the word to Laurence Binyon who was then the editor of a series of slim volumes called *Elkin Matthews' Shilling Garland*.

He offered to publish some of Newbolt's poems in this format and the first edition, hardly bigger than a postcard and containing only twelve poems between simple blue-green paper covers, was available on October 21st 1897. It was entitled *Admirals All* and apart from that poem and *Drake's Drum* it included *San Stefano, The Fighting Téméraire, Hawke, Vae Victis, Vitaï Lampada, A Ballad of John Nicholson, The Guides at Cabul 1879, Ionicus, Minora Sidera* and *Laudabunt Alii*. The first six dealt with heroic episodes in Britain's naval past, two more were concerned with incidents in the Indian Mutiny and the Afghan War, one sang in praise of Devon and the remaining three might be termed scholastic. *Minora Sidera* is a tribute to Sir Leslie Stephen, compiler of the *Dictionary of National Biography, Ionicus* reflects upon the career of the Eton master and poet William Cory, while in *Vitaï Lampada* Newbolt wrote lines which were to reverberate about him for the rest of his life —

There's a breathless hush in the Close tonight —
    Ten to make and the match to win —
A bumping pitch and a blinding light,
    An hour to play and the last man in.
And it's not for the sake of a ribboned coat,
    Or the selfish hope of a season's fame,
But his Captain's hand on his shoulder smote —
    'Play up! play up! and play the game!'

The critic William Archer gave the publication a 'wonderful notice' in *The*

Daily Chronicle, the most literary of the dailies, and *The Times* and the *Spectator* followed suit. There was a mad scramble for the little book and no fewer than twenty-one editions of a thousand copies each were sold in one year.[10]

This was success on a sensational scale. Why? Perhaps the most important factor is that 1897 was a magical year for most people in Britain. 'Ever since the triumphant conclusion of the Napoleonic Wars', writes Jan Morris in *Pax Britannica*, the British 'had seemed to be arbiters of the world's affairs, righting a balance here, dismissing a potentate there, ringing the earth with railways and submarine cables, lending money everywhere, peopling the empty places with men of the British Stock, grandly revenging wrongs, converting pagans, discovering unknown lakes, setting up dynasties, emancipating slaves, winning wars, putting down mutinies, keeping Turks in their place and building bigger and faster battleships. By June 1897 all this vigour and self-esteem, all this famous history, had been fused into an explosive emotional force.'[11] This was the month of Queen Victoria's Diamond Jubilee celebrations when her estimated 372 million subjects all round the world turned to honour the diminutive old lady who had, for as long as almost anyone could remember, reigned over the largest Empire the world had ever known. It was with some reason that English chests swelled with pride to see London's streets filled with gilded processions and all the fanfare of Empire. The secret of Newbolt's success is that his poems expressed what millions really felt, in robust metre free from any taint of Oscar Wildery. These were not the poems of a suspect fop: they were the heartfelt sentiments of a patriotic English gentleman couched in manly ballad style.

Spurred by this success Newbolt wrote twenty-eight new poems within twelve months and published these, together with the original twelve, in 'a more substantial octavo volume' entitled *The Island Race* and available late in 1898. Again, the theme of naval valour ran through seven of them, *The Vigil, Admiral Death, The Quarter-Gunner's Yarn, For a Trafalgar Cenotaph, Craven, Messmates, The Death of Admiral Blake*. Four concerned heroes of the Empire: *Gillespie, Seringapatam, The Gay Gordons, He fell among Thieves*. Another fifteen dealt predominantly with Time, either in the passing of the seasons or man's passage through life. Two, *Clifton Chapel* and *The Echo*, saw school as a microcosm of life:

This is the Chapel: here, my son,
  Your father thought the thoughts of youth,

And heard the words that one by one
The touch of Life has turned to truth.

The Echo had already been published in *The Cliftonian*, set to music by the music master Arthur Peppin and sung by Harry Plunket Greene:

Twice three hundred boys were we,
    Long ago, long ago,
Where the Downs look out to the
    Severn Sea.
  Clifton for aye!
We held by the game and hailed the
    team
For many could play where few
    could dream.
  City of song shall stand alway.

The Island Race was also a triumphant success. Newbolt found himself the centre of attention. 'I was still at the Bar, I had the Digest still to finish, and now I was asked for poems daily by every kind of editor and publisher, I was wearied daily with answering congratulations, replying to questions and refuting misstatements of many kinds in many countries . . . I heard that men like Frederic Myers and Butler of Trinity and Leslie Stephen had been learning me by heart, and that in one expedition after another soldiers were carrying me and reciting me around their camp fires. The time even came when Ministers quoted me in the House, and Bishops recited me in sermons at St. Paul's before the King and Queen.'[12]

Yet it is most sweet for a prophet to be honoured in his own College, as Newbolt put it, and he enjoyed very much returning to give a paper at Corpus for the 200th meeting of the Pelican Essay Club. The talk went well, his audience laughed at the jokes and 'though no one made any reference in words to my having written anything, they poured the most delicate flattery down my neck all the time.'[13] Clifton, too, had taken note of his success. The Headmaster read from *Admirals All* at Commemoration in 1898 and at the O.C. supper on the same occasion Rowland Whitehead, Newbolt's school contemporary and legal colleague who had recently been appointed first Secretary of the O.C. Society, announced with reference to *Admirals All* that he 'was confident that there is not a Cliftonian who does not rejoice at the sudden leap into fame which has attended the publication of that small and unassuming volume.'[14] *The*

Cliftonian magazine reviewing *The Island Race* in its July number was not entirely without criticism. 'We are glad to see that Mr. Newbolt's *Admirals All* has, together with many other poems, been produced in a more permanent form. As the name of the volume implies, most of the pieces tell of the doings of Englishmen — the Island Race — by land, and especially by sea. There are, however, two poems in the book which are of special interest to our readers. One of these, *The Echo*, of Plunket Greene's ballad, appeared first in *The Cliftonian* and is familiar to most of our readers with the tune which Mr. Peppin has written for it. The other poem of special interest to us is that on *Clifton Chapel* . . . The poem is a little disappointing, in that it emphasises only one aspect of the teaching received in Chapel; yet it is the stirring message which Mr. Newbolt is always delivering — to "Play up, play up, and play the game.' ". . . Of the remaining poems, the reviewer thought, 'some of the best are those written in the old ballad style, such as *John Nicholson*, *Gillespie* or *Seringapatam*.'[15]

It is a Clifton tradition to hold House Suppers at the end of the Winter term and Newbolt was invited to North Town's celebrations in December 1898. It was a specially poignant occasion for Wollaston: he was due to retire as Housemaster the following year, so this was his last House Supper. 'Clifton was perfect' Newbolt thought. 'I'm not thinking now of my own particular affairs, for happily though they roared *Drake's Drum* and *Téméraire* at the House Supper, they said very little about my things otherwise. But the place was alive with silent warm congratulation: staid old masters put heavy hands on my shoulder, and boys were introduced to me and flushed and stammered, and at the supper they would hardly let me get on with my speech at all . . . It's a pure marvel, a School, and the intangible invisible thing we call "House-feeling" is about the most wonderful thing in it.'[16] Doubtless it was sentiments such as these which inspired him to write *The Best School of All*, a poem honouring the memory of Clifton, dedicated to Wollaston and published in *The Cliftonian* in the Summer of 1899 to coincide with his retirement.

It's good to see the School we knew,
　　The land of youth and dream,
To greet again the rule we knew
　　Before we took the stream:
Though long we've missed the sight of her,
　　Our hearts may not forget;
We've lost the old delight of her,
　　We keep her honour yet.

We'll honour yet the School we knew,
    The best School of all:
We'll honour yet the rule we knew,
    Till the last bell call.
For, working days or holidays,
    And glad or melancholy days,
They were great days and jolly days
    At the best School of all.

This poem is often thought by its critics to be nauseatingly arrogant, an example of 'alma materism' at its worst. But in all fairness it should be remembered that it was not written as the 'School Song' it eventually became. The verses were finished in March 1899 after Newbolt's visit to North Town House Supper. Now in his late thirties and experiencing success in the world his feelings for Clifton and for Wollaston were warm and loyal and the poem is a tribute to both: but it is not simply a schoolboy's jingoistic cry; it is the musing of a man in early middle age about the experience of Time. Moreover, to take the phrase 'the best School of all' at face value is grossly to underrate Newbolt. He was not so naïve as to make for Clifton any absolute claim to pre-eminence — indeed he was to send his son in a few years time to Winchester. Would it not be a reasonable exaggeration for a child to say that he had 'the best parents in the world' or for a man to declare that he loved 'the most beautiful girl in England'? For a Cliftonian, Newbolt is saying, Clifton is the best school of all because Time, loyalty and experience have created a special bond between the two of them. Furthermore, there is no reason why nostalgia for the teenage years should be seen as an unnatural, maudlin sentiment. George Younghusband, a very level-headed O.C. just a few years older than Newbolt wrote in *The Cliftonian* in 1894 'Looking back at one's school days, perhaps few will deny that the last years are very happy ones indeed. From the hard drudgery of an East-end curacy, from the dead monotony of a clerk's desk in the City, from the poisonous swamps of the West Coast of Africa, the Close at Clifton must seem a paradise.'[17]

Newbolt's poem was only adopted as the official School Song after the failure of some lines of T.E. Brown which were published in *The Cliftonian* just after his death.

Come all ye sons of Clifton
    And gather by her side;
Our Mother sits upon the rocks

And fronts the Severn-tide —
Upon the rocks she keeps her state,
    Our mother strong and free;
She is a Queen, and holds the gate
    Of all the West Countree.[18]

At least nine musical settings of this poem were produced by different hands and one, by C.W. Maudslay, was tried out in 1898: but the words did not have the appeal of Newbolt's poem, especially when Sir Hubert Parry wrote such splendid music for it. Known at first as 'The Old Cliftonians Song', it was first performed at a School Concert in 1908 and soon established itself as 'The School Song'.[20] Most Public School Songs are elegant Latin affairs: Newbolt's poem together with Harrow's *Forty Years On* are probably the two most celebrated English versions of the genre.

'Best School of All' or not the youthful Clifton had continued to prosper during the years of Newbolt's early career. In his sermon at the School's 25th anniversary Percival felt it proper to say 'this school has become looked upon as in some sort one of the great schools of England'.[20] Newbolt's own ties with the School loosened in the 1890's, mainly because he no longer lived in Bristol. Also, many of his main contacts had gone.

Oakeley retired in 1886 and Wilson in 1890, leaving the handsome tower, named after him, as a visible memorial of his Headmastership, which he himself described as 'an age of immense expansion in building, of new timetables, of great development of the College Mission, and of buying new land. But its real and distinctive mark', he added 'is that it was an age of singular internal quiet, changelessness, consolidation and peace.'[21] He became Archdeacon of Manchester, his religious unorthodoxy probably preventing higher preferment. He lived on and on, visiting Clifton often, vigorous in mind and body until death overtook him in his 93rd year, long after the Great War. T.E. Brown, his good friend and fellow Manx enthusiast, retired to his beloved island in 1892 though ironically it was in the middle of an address to the boys of Tait's House in 1897 on the subject of 'The meaning of Clifton' that a blood vessel burst in his brain and he died the same night. The saddest death perhaps was that of Norman Moor, still in his early forties.

Wilson's successor and Clifton's third Headmaster was the Rev. Michael Glazebrook, aged 38. He had been a master at Harrow for ten years and High Master at Manchester Grammar School for two. At Balliol he had read Classics and Maths, though as O.F. Christie suggests, it is possible that many Cliftonians were less impressed by his collection of first classes than by the fact that he was reputedly the first man to clear six feet in the High Jump. A tall, rather forbidding figure, he was Headmaster from 1890 to 1905: the very period when, as many historians of the Public Schools have noted, athleticism and philistinism were the most prominent features of the system. Yet Glazebrook's priorities were the opposite of the prevailing fashion. He strove for academic excellence and, with the building of the Music School and the appointment of Arthur Peppin, he set Clifton on a course that would bring 'the school singing and the standard of instrumental performance to a level that was for a time unrivalled.'[22] At first, all went well. The editor of *The Cliftonian* in October 1892 wrote 'We cannot look back upon the cricket of last Term without feelings of the utmost satisfaction at the achievements of our XI.' Rather as an afterthought he goes on 'We cannot pass over without comment the splendid list of Honours gained by the School during the past year. Fourteen Scholarships were obtained direct from the school, and our success in the Army Examinations was almost unparalleled'.[23] Clifton played a major role in manning the Empire. The Army List of 1898 contained 479 Cliftonians, a certain Douglas Haig among them. In 1900 the *Lahore Civil and Military Gazette* carried an article on 'Which Public School sends out the most men to India.' Research in the India Office files showed that in 1900 as far as the Indian Service was concerned Clifton headed the list with 39, followed by Winchester (38), Charterhouse (35), Marlborough (33), Cheltenham (27), St. Paul's (26), Rugby (23), and Eton (22).[24]

At the turn of the century there is no doubt that Clifton's reputation stood high; and with the very wide distribution of Newbolt's poems about the school it was inevitable that Newbolt and Clifton should in the popular mind become closely linked, even synonymous. And why not? Henry Newbolt's virtues were precisely those that Percival and Wilson had sought to foster in their pupils. Under their leadership Clifton had imparted a strong message to the poet and he in his turn had placed it in the mouths of many thousands of his fellow countrymen.

PART FIVE: 1898–1904

'I was myself a Liberal rooted in the past'

'Ten years is quite long enough to be in any profession,' Robert Bridges told Newbolt firmly on learning that he had been a decade at the Bar.[1] This rather tied in with Newbolt's own views because he found his legal work tedious. But how else was he to feed a wife and a growing family? That was his reaction before the success of his poems: by 1898 he had more or less taken the decision to drop the Law and risk earning his living as a full-time writer. He was also able to afford a move to a larger and more elegant house in Earl's Terrace where dinner-parties were frequent and the rooms were increasingly filled with the entertaining conversation of London's literary figures. He began another book, *Stories from Froissart*, followed by a sequel *Froissart in Britain*: neither was an original book but extracts from Lord Berners' translation of Froissart's *Chronicles*. Newbolt was a great admirer of this fourteenth century historian who 'searched diligently for facts, but the value of his narrative is an artistic value. The great fact which emerges from his workshop is the mingling of the beautiful and the fierce in the civilisation of his time: and his condonation of the ferocity for the sake of the beauty.'[2] In his historical books Newbolt was himself to become something of a latter-day Froissart, searching diligently for the facts, using prose not far short of poetry, blind to neither the ferocity nor the beauty of warfare. There is a passage in his introduction to *Stories from Froissart* which exactly describes the sense in which Newbolt viewed warfare as 'a game.' 'For the knights of England and France, as for Nelson, to be fighting was to be "in the full tide of happiness", and I do not doubt that their descendants, for some generations yet, will feel the same stirring of the blood. It will be well if they frankly own to it, taking care that at the same time they keep alive the soldierly instincts of discipline, loyalty, and fair play; that the new men-of-arms, like the old, look with sympathy on all human fortitude, and with tenderness on all human suffering: that they learn, like their ancestors, to fight without hatred, to conquer without insolence, and to meet death without terror; to think of honour as the true self-interest, and of nobility as the right to serve.'[3]

The new century bought with it an offer which greatly affected the course of Newbolt's career. The publisher John Murray suggested that he might like to edit a new literary magazine. 'To no-one would we entrust the Editorship more readily than to yourself', Murray wrote, 'for the position you have won in the world of letters, coupled with your own personality . . . will go far to ensure a wide popular reception for any literary work which you may undertake.'⁴ They agreed upon a title, *The Monthly Review* and the first number appeared in October 1900. For four years Newbolt worked full time to attract interesting articles for the magazine and this activity brought him into close contact with leading figures in the literary and also the political world. The very first to be approached was his Clifton contemporary Roger Fry whose earliest lectures were published in *The Monthly Review*. Another O.C. who wrote for the first issue was the astronomer Herbert Turner who reviewed the recently published *Collected Poems of T.E. Brown*. Poetry was bound to be a special interest and Newbolt persuaded Robert Bridges and W.B. Yeats to write for him. He also 'discovered' Walter de la Mare who had sent in some poems which Newbolt recognised to be of fine quality. They were to remain firm friends for thirty years: Newbolt eventually rescued him from a dreary job as clerk in an oil company by using his influence to secure money for him from the King's Bounty.⁵ In 1904 Newbolt reviewed Thomas Hardy's epic poem *The Dynasts*, hailing it as a masterpiece, not everybody's view at the time. Hardy was delighted. 'A review from a practising poet' he wrote later 'is worth hundreds of pages from a mere critic.'⁶ Thus began another friendship conducted by letter and in long conversations at the Savile Club.

John Murray had probably assumed that Newbolt's interests would have been almost exclusively literary but from the first it became clear that his enthusiasm for politics had found a new outlet. Murray was a Conservative; Newbolt described himself as 'a Liberal rooted in the Past.' Liberals everywhere were encouraged to support the new *Monthly Review*. 'Politically', declared *The Huddersfield Examiner* 'the magazine's Liberalism may be described as philosophically Imperialistic — a form of Imperialism which should not frighten the least expansive Liberal, though not all Liberals will accept the teachings of the Editor.'⁷ The main issues of the day — Free Trade, Reform of the Army system, the State of the Navy, the Future of the Liberal party — all were discussed in *The Monthly Review* and Newbolt became firmly associated with Liberal politics as well as the confidant of men like Haldane, Buxton and Grey. In this he was doubtless helped by the fact that Sidney Buxton was an Old Cliftonian of the Percival generation, while two of Sir Edward Grey's brothers had been at Clifton with Frank Newbolt. All during his time at *The Monthly Review* the

Liberals were in opposition but after they came to power in 1905 Newbolt found that he had many friends in high places. On the other hand he never seems particularly to have befriended Asquith, whose sharp-tongued brother 'the Pup' was a Clifton housemaster.

One of the most important events during Newbolt's time with *The Monthly Review* was the South African War which began in October 1899 and lasted until peace was signed in May 1902. The two Boer republics of the Transvaal and the Orange Free State had a population, as Lloyd George was quick to point out, which 'did not exceed that of Flintshire and Denbighshire'.[8] Here, in Britain's determination to subdue them with an army of about half a million, was 'the game' of war envisaged in Newbolt's poems, a romantic war fought in sunshine on open plains with gloriously costumed cavalry charging, it was hoped, to victory. 'The great majority of us', he wrote later 'saw no reason to disbelieve in the goodness of our cause, though our feelings drew a conscientious line between Chamberlain and Rhodes, the negotiator and privateer. War was cleverly and deliberately forced upon us by President Kruger's ultimatum, and from that moment we felt that the question of right or wrong must be put away until the struggle had been decided.'[9]

It was to be rather more of a struggle than most people on the British side had bargained for. Yet following so closely the success of Newbolt's patriotic poems the war made those poems even more relevant and focused attention on the author and, to a lesser extent, on Clifton. An example of this is the poem entitled *Sed Miles, Sed pro Patria* (the last line of *Clifton Chapel*) which was published in the Keswick School Magazine in December 1899:[10]

> What tho' we have not there one hostage yet
> Where cold grey *veldt* and grey cold heavens form
> A shadowy background for heroic deeds!
> Tho', children of one summer, we alone
> Amongst the schools of England cannot prove
> Our school-hood there amid the splendid shocks
> And patient, grand endurances of war!
> Have we no share in Clifton's pride, who sends
> Her hundred forth and wins new strength of life
> From out their death, fresh spur to fellowship
> From each lone outpost of the Empress Queen,
> Guarding far off her honour and the school's
> In uttermost allegiance? . . .

The 'hundred' referred to in the poem is probably a poetic rounding of the 85 names mentioned in the October 1899 '*Cliftonian*' as having set out for South Africa. By February 1900 there were 200 serving and the total number was to be 347, almost all officers, though the one Cliftonian V.C. of this war was a Sergeant, H.R. Martineau.[11] The news of the relief of Mafeking was celebrated at Clifton by an assembly of the whole school in the quadrangle at 11.00 am. The National Anthem was sung and the boys were let off the next two lessons. Several O.C.'s sent in lively accounts of their adventures in the War, many evocative of the Kipling style. More Newboltian is this extract from the O.C. Chronicle: 'A distinguished Old Cliftonian writes that he is probably the only ex-German officer on our side of the scrimmage; another writes with patriotic exaggeration that the blue, white and green of the O.C. blazer has become a common object in South African scenery; another played in the first cricket match at Bloemfontein but as he only made two runs we do not give his name.'[12]

Newbolt wrote three poems during the Boer war, on his now well-established theme of the game on the Close and the game on the battlefield. The first was written in November 1899 and called *The School Fellow* —

> Our game was his but yesteryear;
>   We wished him back; we could not know
> The selfsame hour we missed him here
>   He led the line that broke the foe.

In May 1901 he produced *The School at War* which tells of an army sleeping fitfully before a battle, dreaming of times past —

> We heard beyond the desert night
>   The murmur of the fields we knew,
> And our swift souls with one delight
>   Like homing swallows Northward flew.
>
> We played again the immortal games,
>   And grappled with the fierce old friends,
> And cheered the dead undying names,
>   And sang the song that never ends.

Third came the poem *Commemoration*, written in July 1901, a week after the annual celebrations at Clifton where a sad note was introducd because the list of Cliftonians who had died in the war was considered too long to read out. In the poem Newbolt reflects on bygone days in Chapel when 'the sermon rolled and rolled' but the thoughts of the youthful audience were far away —

> For some were already away to the hazardous pitch,
>   Or lining the parapet wall,
> And some were in glorious battle, or great and rich,
>   Or throned in a college hall:
> And among the rest was one like my own young phantom,
>   Dreaming for ever beyond my utmost call.

These three Clifton poems, together with *The Best School of All* were published in a new volume entitled *The Sailing of the Long Ships* which appeared in 1902. Of some thirty poems, about half are concerned with the war and the sacrifices made for it; many of the rest sing of History and the Sea, including one of Newbolt's best poems, *The Old Superb* which appeared in later editions.

As the casualty list lengthened a large number of Old Cliftonians came together in the summer of 1901 to discuss the question of a Memorial. The Chairman was that white-haired Patriarch of the Clifton world, John Percival, now a Bishop. He had left Trinity College in 1887 to revitalize Rugby School and then accepted the Bishopric of Hereford from a Liberal Prime Minister, Lord Rosebery, in 1895, the year in which he also became Chairman of the Clifton Council. He chaired the Committee elected to arrange for a Memorial and among the ten O.C. members were Henry Newbolt and his school contemporaries Rowland Whitehead and John McTaggart. In due course they accepted the overall plan of the architect W.S. Paul who had been at Clifton in its opening years. This was for a sculpture on a pedestal to stand 'on a semi-circular platform in line with the centre of the School buildings, but projecting beyond the terrace wall so as not to interfere with the view of the Chapel . . . On the pedestal would be placed a figure in bronze, emblematical of "patriotism" '.[13] So much was agreed: the difficult question was — what sort of figure? Some favoured a soldier in contemporary uniform: others, surely led by Newbolt, advocated a knight in fourteenth century armour, the uniform of Chivalry. There were those who did not think much of the idea. 'I understand' wrote *'O'erpeering Truth* in *The Cliftonian* 'that it has been irrevocably decided that the Memorial is not to be in any way connected with the Chapel, but is to take the form of a hardy warrior overlooking the Close, who, if he has not to face volleys of bullets, must at least run the risk of being peppered by stray cricket balls; but even if this be the case, is it necessary that the hero should be clad in the obsolete panoply of a bygone generation? Was there any occasion during the late war on which a *kopje* was scaled, a river forded, or a withering fire endured by warriors who were encumbered by heavy defensive armour?'[14]

Many Cliftonians agreed with this point of view so the Committee commissioned the sculptor Alfred Drury to produce two small models, one in medieval, the other in modern guise. It seems that 'after considerable discussion' in which it can be guessed that the patient yet courteously determined and powerfully persuasive arguments of Henry Newbolt carried much weight, 'a majority was found to be in favour of the Gothic pedestal and the figure of St. George.'[15] It was, surely, a happy decision. Drury produced a quite magnificent bronze statue which despite the effect it has of appearing to leak green ink onto its pedestal remains to-day one of the visual glories of Clifton. The sculptor described his creation thus 'The armour is of the period of the late fourteenth century; the shield is Gothic, with the Cross of St. George on it; the handle of the sword is surmounted with a figure emblematical of Love; the figure of Christ is surmounted by a symbol of the Holy Ghost, intended to represent the descent of the spirit of God or the Word of God; the hilt takes the form of an anchor of Hope. In the head of St. George I have endeavoured to express his character of Fortitude and Virtue without effeminacy'.[16] And so he has: if there ever was a visible representation of muscular Christianity, manly Virtue, the Victorian educator's ideal realised, this surely is it. Moreover St. George is essentially a Newbolt hero, fashioned in medieval form yet embodying timeless values. The Portland stone pedestal on which the statue stands bears a bronze tablet on each side: three of these are inscribed with the names and ranks of the forty-three Old Cliftonians who fell in the war. On the fourth, facing the Close, is engraved Newbolt's tribute:

> Clifton, remember these thy sons who fell
> Fighting far over sea;
> For they in a dark hour remembered well
> Their warfare learned of thee.

The Memorial was formally unveiled at Commemoration in 1904 by Lord Methuen, the General blamed at the time for the failure at Magersfontein. Newbolt had written an editorial article in *The Monthly Review* seeking to defend him to some extent. Methuen wrote gratefully in reply, ending 'Of course all was not perfect — nothing in life is. I had best not have sent in the Gordons when I did — too soon. One is so much wiser when the fog lifts'.[17] At the Clifton ceremony Methuen emphasised the fact that all who had died were volunteers and urged the boys before him not to be slow in offering their service in all walks of life. He also spoke of two Cliftonians not present, Colonel Birdwood, 'the beau ideal of what a British officer and an English gentleman should be,' and Colonel Haig 'of whom as a comrade he might say the British Army was proud, as a man who had zeal, ability, and a charm of manner.'[18]

Twenty-eight years later another generation of Cliftonians would stand on a similar spot to see unveiled, after all, a statue in modern uniform. But take away the Field-Marshal's peaked hat and Douglas Haig's moustache, and the face is the face of St. George.

PART SIX: 1904–1914

'These were good years for me, and I enjoyed them to the full'

Newbolt and *The Monthly Review* parted company in the summer of 1904. He wrote of a 'decline from its earlier prosperity', the result, paradoxically, of the fact that very popular editions had to be reprinted to meet demand and this was uneconomic. Another problem was the political climate: as a General Election came closer Newbolt felt inclined to take an increasingly partisan line in favour of the Liberals. This was unwelcome to the Tory Murray, as Newbolt well knew, and his offer to resign in June was courteously accepted. The release from so demanding a commitment was by no means unwelcome, especially as a new project very close to Newbolt's heart now presented itself. He determined to write a history of the Battle of Trafalgar to mark its centenary in 1905. His grandfather's involvement with Nelson's fleet had excited him from childhood and he eagerly threw himself into the research for his first piece of serious historical writing, thrilling to the touch of primary sources. In the Record Office he read the Captain's journal and Master's log of every ship in the fleet and came to a spectacular conclusion. The traditional view was that Trafalgar had been won by an attack in two columns led by Nelson and Collingwood, in line astern: but the sources showed that Collingwood changed to line abreast before engaging the enemy. That is the message of the book, which also contains twenty-six poems about the battle, six of Newbolt's own included. The best chapters, he thought, were written at Barlaston in the house of Josiah Wedgwood who had been at Clifton a decade after Newbolt and wanted his advice about the world of Liberal politics. 'Between Nelsonian tactics and political strategy', Newbolt wrote of this episode, 'I had a bracing time on that Staffordshire hilltop, and was happy to feel that two Old Cliftonians were all the time building up a friendship that would last their lives'.[1]

The book was well received and Joseph Conrad, whom Newbolt was trying to help out of financial difficulties, wrote to him: 'Of course the tone, the expression, the feeling are all what we expect from you. To my mind (not skilled, of course, in these matters but still a seaman's mind) your discussion of the tactics seems to settle the question.'[2] In fact controversy persisted until, in 1912, after a long correspondence in *The Times* about the Trafalgar tactics, the Admiralty set up a three man Committee to report on the matter. Two members were Admirals, Sir Cyprian Bridge and Sir Reginald Custance, the latter a good friend of Newbolt's. The third was the Regius Professor of Modern History at Oxford, Charles Firth, who had gone from Clifton to begin a distinguished academic career the year before Newbolt entered the school. Their report delighted him. 'My estimate of the evidence, my marshalling of it, my conclusion on the principal issue, and even my amateur plan of the action, were all unequivocally confirmed.'[3] *The Year of Trafalgar* established Newbolt as a serious historian of naval affairs, a voice heard with respect at the Admiralty.

His next book, published in 1906, was a historical romance, *The Old Country*, a story inspired by Orchardleigh, the beautiful and historic house of Newbolt's father-in-law. Stephen Bulmer, a young novelist, stays at 'Gardenleigh' and falls in love with Aubrey, the daughter of the house. He reads a history of the place, then, while wandering among the ruins on the estate he drifts into the past, becoming part of the Marland family who lived there in the fourteenth century. There is much dispute between a Lollard priest and the Bishop of Exeter: the son of the house returns with tales of the Battle of Poitiers and Stephen eventually flits back into the twentieth century and the arms of his Aubrey. There is little action but a good deal of intellectual conversation not only on the themes of Time, Chivalry and Romance, but also Religion and the 'Protestant v Catholic' argument. It is one of the few books of Newbolt's to contain a strong religious element and it was dedicated to Cosmo Lang, then Bishop of Stepney, a friend from Oxford Union days. The book contains many interesting ideas of a philosophic nature; the style is poetic, and Time is overcome as the fourteenth and the twentieth centuries blend together.

It was in the September term of 1906 that Newbolt's son Francis first went to school at Winchester. In view of the central place Clifton had held — and continued to hold — in Henry Newbolt's affections it is a puzzling feature of him, perhaps *the* most puzzling feature, that he did not send his only son there. He nowhere explains exactly why, so reasons must be sought. In the first place he admired the historical associations of the 'second capital of medieval England' with which he had ancestral connections — the Mayor of Winchester in the year of the Spanish Armada had been a certain Charles Newbolt. In 1903 he had persuaded his mother to move from Surrey to a house on St. Giles's Hill in Winchester: there she would be well placed to entertain her grandson and indeed

Winchester society in general, rather in the way she had done at Clifton in the Worcester Crescent days. Moreover the Newbolts would be able to visit their son and the College very conveniently whenever time permitted.

The young Newbolt had been sent in 1902 to Horris Hill, a Preparatory School whose Headmaster was Alfred Evans, Captain of the XI at Clifton in his father's time. This seemed to suggest an eventual transition to Clifton. But Henry Newbolt had recommended Horris Hill to Quiller-Couch whose son Bevil befriended Francis Newbolt: *he* went to Winchester, which may explain why Francis wanted to follow him two years later. But why did Bevil go to Winchester? What was wrong with Clifton?

The school had recently gone through a bad patch. Although academic results remained very good it seems that morale was low. The rugby season of 1902 was disappointing. According to *The Cliftonian*, 'want of physique, a temporary depression in the development of the School, seems to be the disadvantage under which we labour'.[3] In 1903 the XV lost all its matches, prompting the ominous comment 'the degeneration of our football cannot be ascribed to want of physique, for we suspect that the fault lies deeper still — in lack of energy.'[4] In the same issue the Captain of Clifton Rowing Club seized his opportunity: 'I am told that the physique of the School is deteriorating. If this is so, why does Clifton not become a rowing school?'[5] Unlikely though this alleged physical degeneration seems there must have been something in it to prompt Glazebrook's successor to announce 'I do not consider the average Clifton boy as well set up as he might be.'[6] When Glazebrook became Headmaster in 1891 the total number of boys in the school was 629. From 1898 onwards there was a steady annual decline to 528 in 1905. In view of the fact that four years after his departure numbers recovered to 654 it must be assumed that the personality of the Headmaster was to blame. He was not much liked by boys or masters, several of whom left for posts elsewhere. No-one doubted his industry or integrity and the Council backed him when he first offered to resign because of falling numbers: but he had the austerity of Percival without the charisma and he lacked the spontaneous humanity of Wilson. He was a man who, to judge from his sermons and public pronouncements, appeared to be stern, sanctimonious, and dull. The council agreed to accept his resignation in 1905 and he was appointed a Canon of Ely Cathedral. Away from the responsibilities of Clifton he mellowed a good deal and 'was in great demand as a preacher at Westminster Abbey and other famous churches.'[7] When his portrait by

William Strang was unveiled, *The Cliftonian* commented that 'opinions vary as to its merits',[8] a verdict perhaps equally applicable to the sitter.

Newbolt might, for these reasons, have felt uneasy about sending Francis to Clifton but he need not really have worried, for the Council found exactly the right man to succeed Glazebrook. The Rev. Albert Augustus David, a tall vigorous bachelor in his late thirties, had taught at Bradfield and Rugby before taking up a Fellowship at Queen's Oxford. He was at Clifton for only four years before being whisked off to Rugby as Headmaster and eventually to Liverpool as Bishop. It was long enough, however, to restore the health, morale and numbers of the school. Newbolt must have taken the measure of the man when he attended the Christmas Concert in David's first term to hear Harry Plunket Greene sing C.V. Stanford's settings of his *Songs of the Sea*, conducted by the composer himself.

David's solution to the 'physique' problem appears to have been to ordain that all boys should sleep soundly between the hours of ten and seven, and to introduce Physical Training and Swedish Drill. He also felt that the Close was inadequate as a games field and urged the purchase of 48 acres of land on the other side of Clifton Gorge. He made important changes in the curriculum, encouraging science, modern languages and 'civics', and he supported an ambitious scheme to enlarge the Chapel in time for the School's Jubilee celebrations in 1912. Within months of David's arrival at Clifton, compliments were showered upon him. He was 'sunny', 'buoyant', a 'shrewd man of business': at Commemoration in 1907 Sir Herbert Warren described him as 'a versatile, strenuous, high-minded, capable, modest man.'[9] Indeed, for Clifton's good he was too successful. Dolefully *The Cliftonian* recorded in the term after he had left for Rugby: 'not only have we lost our Headmaster, but the Marlborough match as well'.[10]

'On a chart of my life', Newbolt wrote, 'the course of the year 1907 would be marked as a very sharp turn.'[11] This was because he and his family moved from London to a house in the countryside near Salisbury. It was an experiment: their friend the sculptor Henry Furse lived alone in a sprawling old manor house in the village of Netherhampton and they had agreed to set up a joint household with him. It was also a risk, for the Newbolts liked their London home: but Netherhampton House became for them a kind of paradise, their haven for twenty-seven years. Founded in Elizabethan times it had expanded to match the escalating rank of its various owners: by Newbolt's day the main facade, looking south, had the aspect of an eighteenth century villa: behind lay long, low wings of earlier date. There were extensive gardens and views across the Wiltshire downs. It was exactly the place to appeal to Newbolt's sense of beauty and history, the beauty not ostentatious, the history all-pervading. And there were ghosts: one who beheaded his wife at intervals in Newbolt's study, another who dropped rings into a china basin in his dressing room and a third, that of Harriet Grove, more welcome perhaps because she had known and loved the poet Shelley.[12] The shared household with Henry Furse worked well — so well that within seven years Newbolt's daughter Celia, a poet in her own right, married Furse's son Ralph. The main living-room was the hall, panelled the colour of old ivory; the chief occupations were lively conversation, Patience, and, for the summer months, bowls on the lawn. Newbolt's work-room was nicknamed 'Noah's Ark' and has been described by Ralph Furse. 'A glass door led from the hall to a panelled staircase, with broad shallow treads of polished oak. From the landing steep, twisty stairs mounted to Newbolt's study. This was a long low white attic, facing south towards the Downs. A huge transverse beam, a foot high, divided the floor. Two pairs of white rafters at intervals supported the sloping roof. These and the four deep set, round headed windows gave the room something of a look of a frigate's gundeck; an effect which was heightened by a small round porthole of a window at the far end, and was not lost upon the author of *Drake's Drum*. Newbolt worked at a small kitchen table covered with a plain blue cloth and surmounted by one of those old square sloping writing desks. Beside this stood a vast accordion file which played a notable part in his scheme of life. Extremely methodical in business and punctual in all correspondence that mattered, he had a masterly way with trivial or inconvenient letters. They just went unanswered into that file for a month or two and by that time had mostly answered themselves.'[13] At this table, in this room, most of Newbolt's considerable literary output was to take shape.

The year after the move to Netherhampton (1908) was, Newbolt thought, 'one of my most strenuous years.' In May Admiral Sir Reginald Custance invited him to spend a week with the Channel Fleet on board HMS *Hibernia*, not only because of his reputation as a naval poet, but because of his recent interest in a new range-finding system for naval guns. He enjoyed the experience immensely and was shown even the most secret technicalities of the ship. He was amused to discover later that Admiral Fisher had taken the precaution of having him spied upon by security agents. In due course he published *Songs of the Fleet*, a number of lyric poems recording his impressions of a memorable week. This year also saw the publication of a slim volume entitled *Clifton Chapel and other school poems* in which some of his already published Clifton verses were collected, together with a few new ones, such as the *Epistle dedicated to Colonel Francis Younghusband*, a school contemporary already distinguished as a soldier, explorer and statesman. In the poem Newbolt recalls how the two of them used to strive for the first place in the long distance races, Younghusband usually winning. Since then both men had run the race on different courses, though still united by past friendship and a common aim:

> The past we love not for its being past,
> But for its hope and ardour forward cast:
> The victories of our youth we count but gain
> Only because they steeled our hearts to pain,
> And hold no longer even Clifton great
> Save as she schooled our wills to serve the State.

It was increasingly as an expert on naval affairs that Newbolt was able 'to serve the State'. A major issue in 1908 was that of England's role at sea: Campbell-Bannerman's Government seemed to favour disarmament but many, Newbolt among them, were worried by the German naval threat. 'It was a question that concerned everyone and was endlessly discussed', Newbolt wrote. 'I was constantly being invited to consult with such men as Grey, Haldane, Corbett, Sydenham, William White, Custance, and Carlyon Bellairs, and I often lamented that I had no longer the forces of the old *Monthly Review* at my command!'[14]

Newbolt did not have the salary of an editor to command, for that matter, and literary work, though doubtless a pleasure, was also a financial necessity. Encouraged by the success of *The Old Country* he embarked upon another historical novel, *The New June*, placed like its forerunner in the 14th century. The central character is John Marland, grandson of Sir Henry Marland of Gardenleigh: he becomes squire to Thomas Holland, a close relative of Richard II, and is soon caught up in the dangerous politics of the reign, travelling with his master to Jerusalem, Venice and Milan, fighting for Richard II against Bolingbroke and only after the death of his King marrying his lady-love, a supporter of the other side. The historical descriptions are scholarly and convincing and the account of the burial of Richard II's favourite, Robert de Vere, is very fine: in some ways Newbolt most proclaims himself a poet in his prose. Again an autobiographical element is present in this novel because some of the scenes are centred on

5 Emily (Milly) Newbolt, aged nine.

6 A drawing of the College from *The Graphic*, August 28th 1875.

7 Charles Hansom's original concept from the first prospectus.

8 Masters in 1877.

9 'He had the grace of a marble statue'. A bust of John Percival, 1880, by the distinguished sculptor Thomas Woolner, R.A., now in the East Cloister, Clifton College.

10 G.H. Wollaston, Newbolt's housemaster in North Town. 'I had only one mother, and one Wollaston'.

11 Above: The Chapel in 1887.

12 Below: Cricket on the Close in 1890.

13 Henry Newbolt as a member of the Clifton College Cadet Corps — his only spell in uniform.

14 Newbolt (right) with his brother Francis (centre) and a friend.

15 Above: The Front Quadrangle, Corpus Christi College, Oxford.

16 Right: Henry Newbolt, aged 27.

Mount Grace, a medieval Yorkshire Priory which the Newbolts were able to use for many years as a holiday retreat. The book was a critical and financial success though Newbolt's decision to dispense with old-fashioned language and make 'his young knights and squires as much as possible like modern undergraduates',[15] as one reviewer put it, caused healthy controversy and set something of a fashion. It also established him as a Richard II enthusiast and he was soon commissioned to edit the Shakespeare play for a Clarendon Press volume.

For his third novel, *The Twymans*, published in 1911 Newbolt chose not only modern times but selected as the main character none other than himself. Many novelists draw freely from their own experience but it is perhaps surprising that Newbolt, not a man given to self-advertisement, should have decided to present the story of his early life through the medium of this admittedly rather charming tale. 'Percival Twyman', he calls himself; Percival in homage to his Headmaster, or to the chivalrous knight? His family is faithfully described and his years at Caistor, Clifton and Oxford are recounted: names are changed but pen portraits of characters he encountered are unmistakable. Only at Oxford does fantasy supplant reality, for there Percival befriends Edward Donelly and his sister Althea. They are the grandchildren of Sir William Twyman, a baronet whose estate in Wiltshire was granted to a common ancestor by Henry VIII. Gradually Percival learns that because of the laws of entail he has a better claim to Sir William's title than the Donellys for they are the children of the baronet's daughter and he has no son. This throws Percival into a moral dilemma as he is a friend of Edward's and is falling in love with Althea. A neat, melodramatic solution would have been for Edward to die of consumption and for Percival to marry Althea, but Newbolt rises above the temptation. The conclusion is less spectacular, though honourable to all parties. *The Twymans* is certainly not a great novel but it is most elegantly written and, for those interested in the autobiographical aspect, fascinating. The book paid homage as we have seen to Percival (Dr Cumberland) and Clifton (Downton) and reinforced Newbolt's association with the school in the mind of the reading public.

The Twymans was published in time for the Jubilee celebrations at Clifton. In 1910, the year when King Edward VII died and King George V succeeded, John Edward King was appointed Headmaster of the College. After the youthful David the Council had chosen an experienced man who had already been Headmaster of two schools. King was, moreover, an Old Cliftonian who had left the school in 1877, the year after Newbolt entered it: no doubt he remembered 'Johnny' King as one of the heroes of the

Sixth. In this Jubilee year the skyline of the College had been significantly altered — most thought enhanced — by Sir Charles Nicholson's inspired enlargement of the Chapel, now crowned by a polygonal lantern reminiscent of Ely Cathedral. Another visual change was the abandonment by the boys of black coats in favour of grey flannel suits.

The first important event of Clifton's Jubilee Year, 1912, was the visit to the school of George V and Queen Mary. The King's carriage stopped, appropriately enough, by the statue of St. George and he was presented with a volume containing a loyal address. In a short speech of reply he said:

'The steady progress of your school since its foundation fifty years ago has earned for you a place among the great Public Schools of England, of which you may ever be proud, and I am glad that our visit coincides with an event so memorable in your annals as the celebration of your Jubilee.

'The foundations of a man's career are laid in his school-days and you who are being educated here are to be congratulated on the opportunities open to you to equip your minds and bodies for the work which awaits you in the larger world, into which you will carry with you the spirit and traditions of Clifton.'[16]

Shortly afterwards the School Corps staged a very elaborate Field Day with the help of several other school contingents. At the end of the day all the participants assembled on the newly acquired Beggar's Bush Fields to be addressed by Field-Marshal Lord Roberts.

'I was not at Clifton College myself', he said, 'because it did not exist in my school days, but I lived so many years of my early life in Clifton that I, of course, take a great interest in the College on that account. I know what good work Clifton College has done, and how many good fellows it has turned out. Some of them I have known very well after they left. According to the list the Headmaster has given me, I see that over one thousand boys have gone into the Army, and some ninety into the Navy. Then, of course, in other professions Clifton has done well.

'I know Douglas Haig, one of my youngest and best officers. Then Clifton College has sent out Birdwood and the two Younghusbands, both friends of mine, and General Heath, who was in charge of the operations today. Then there is Newbolt, the man who wrote those splendid words "Play up! Play the game." '[17]

Later still there was the School Supper at which the Head of School, F.N. Tribe, quoted the 'School Song' extensively in his speech. A concert followed, but 'half-way through the proceedings our first Headmaster, the Bishop of Hereford, came into the room with Mr. King, and both were enthusiastically cheered. The former spoke a few encouraging words to us, giving us, as a last farewell, the words written by our own poet: "Play up, play up, and play the game." '[18]

It was Newbolt's Jubilee too. Both Clifton and he were fifty years old and his mind doubtless dwelt upon that fact as he attended one or other of these occasions. This was the year in which he published his volume *Poems New and Old*, a collection of most of his verses to date, with a few new ones. It really marked the end of his productive phase as a poet. Only one more volume of verse, *St. George's Day*, was published in his lifetime. As a writer of patriotic poems he was effectively silenced by the horrors of the Great War.

PART SEVEN: 1914–1928

'It is so absurdly like a schoolboy's game'

All Newbolt had ever written about War presupposed that strict rules should govern its conduct. He had not lived, so far, in an age of atrocities — the 'Pax Britannica' had seen to that. In his study of History, whether the conflicts of the fourteenth century or the Napoleonic wars, he found chivalry and civilised standards among the soldiers. This was probably an idealised view: there are plenty of atrocities in History, especially in the context of ideological or religious warfare. But for Newbolt, war was 'the game', formidable, dangerous, yet essentially honourable. Imagine, then, his dismay to be seated at dinner next to an apparently civilised and charming German diplomat who spoke of Oxford as 'a place of unique charm, an irreplaceable treasure', yet in a future war 'one of England's most vulnerable spots, perhaps the very first to be marked for destruction'. Newbolt argued in vain 'that no civilised enemy would attack an unfortified city, which was a great artistic monument, and a seat of learning'. To this the German replied with serious courtesy that he had every hope that the danger might be avoided, but that like all true Germans he recognised the predominance of his own country as the only test of civilisation, the only motive of moral action. He quoted 'the fundamental truth' that 'the State is Power' and the 'fundamental principle' that 'what is good for the pursuit of Power is proper and necessary'. Newbolt had been familiar with the ideas of Machiavelli from the time of discussions at Clifton with his friend Lawrence Burd, a future editor of *The Prince*, but he found it difficult to make reply: 'a kind of horror had suddenly taken hold of me, a nightmare vision of a new order of the world against which it was useless to protest a struggle'.[1] Less than twelve months after this incident, war was a reality.

'What is fame?' Newbolt wrote in August 1914 to Lady Hylton, a long-standing friend and collaborator. 'Certainly a sale of 70,000 copies is not! *The Vigil* is being quoted, sung, recited and reprinted from one end of the country to another, and I have letters of thanks by every post, but so far not one — even among my friends — has observed that it was published in 1898 and has appeared in all three of my collected volumes since then!'[2]

The point was that it captured the mood of the moment —

England! where the sacred flame
  Burns before the inmost shrine,
Where the lips that love thy name
  Consecrate their hopes and thine,
Where the banners of thy dead
Weave their shadows overhead,
Watch beside thine arms tonight,
Pray that God defend the Right.

At 52 Newbolt was beyond an age suitable for enlistment but his son-in-law Ralph Furse and his son Francis were soon off to the front, Ralph with 'two lovely horses'. To his son Newbolt wrote 'I hope you may get into the Oxfords; they're among the most famous of the Peninsular Regiments. They were the 43rd and 52nd under Picton and Pack, the famous 'Light Division', and it was the 52nd who charged the left flank of the French Guard at Waterloo and drove them all across the field — the crowning stroke of the battle.'[3] Francis did indeed join the Oxfordshire and Buckinghamshire Light Infantry, though he was invalided home after suffering shell-concussion in 1915 and spent the rest of the War as an instructor. For five years then, the Newbolts were never without fear of the dreaded telegram. A month before the war ended Newbolt wrote 'My own terrors — for my country, for F and R — have become so familiar that they no longer haunt me. Certainly the boys may yet be taken; and that would be a sorrow I can't even imagine: but till the moment comes my nerves of fear are quiet — simply from fatigue.'[4]

Among Newbolt's earliest letters to his son at the front was one dated January 14th, 1915 which began 'Yesterday I went to see the King, and he said "Sir . . . Henry" very solemnly and slowly, and I saw also a whole crowd of fellows in khaki, and some of them were wounded and had slings and crutches, and eight of them got V.C's and about forty got D.S.O's.'[5] The Prime Minister, that brother of a Clifton housemaster, had suggested to Newbolt that he should accept a knighthood while they were both guests at a dinner party some months before the war. We may assume that to a man with Newbolt's high regard for knights and chivalry the honour did not come lightly. It marked twin achievements: those of a poet and man of letters with a national reputation, and those of a man committed to Liberal politics and service of the State — a service consisting mainly of giving sound advice to his political friends when they asked for it.

During the war years Newbolt produced ten books, only one of them poetry. Four were adventure stories for boys, published by Longmans. They all follow the same pattern, telling the tale of heroic episodes from different periods of history, and their aim is to evoke both an interest in the past and an enthusiasm for manly exploits. *The Book of the Blue Sea* (1914) tells of five young naval officers, two of them members of his own family, around the time of Trafalgar, an account of which is also given. *The Book of the Thin Red Line* (1915) deals with military exploits in the Napoleonic period, the Indian Mutiny, and the American Civil War. The main characters in each story are young: as Newbolt states in the Preface 'all of them were boys, and they took war as boys take their games, with a mixture of fun and deadly earnest: like Ulysses they enjoyed greatly and suffered greatly.'[6]

In *Tales of the Great War* Newbolt dealt with recent events. The first story tells of 'a subaltern' (unnamed, but based on his own son) who goes to the front in 1914 straight from Public School and Oxford. He experiences life in the trenches, Hill 60, the Battle of Ypres, gas attacks. Eventually he becomes a bad case of shell concussion and is invalided home. The Newbolt theme is still strong here. 'I have heard C.O's say that the useful new subalterns in this war have come mostly from the Public Schools and Universities, and many of the best of them have been those who were accustomed to leading in games.'[7] 'It is all so absurdly like a schoolboy's game', the subaltern writes home, 'in which the main idea is tit for tat and a bit more if you can do it.'[8] This could have been a portrait of almost any of the many thousands of young men who had gone to the front from Clifton and other schools. Every wartime issue of *The Cliftonian* carried a lengthy section entitled *Vitae Prodigi Patriae Profuere*, with short biographies of those who had lost their lives. Newbolt's book also describes the Battles of Coronel, the Falklands and Jutland, as well as the Zeppelin War in the air. And he finds a modern hero, Sir Horace Smith-Dorrien, prominent at Mons, the Marne, the Aisne , the fight for Calais. 'He is the real hero of this war for us, as Father Joffre and Castelnau and Pétain are for the French. He is the General whom the army will remember.'[9] And what makes a good General? 'What was needed first of all was character. This is where games are the miniature of War and of any active life. We have all known good cricketers who could see clearly and make beautiful shots when nothing much depended on them, but who lost their form when a rot set in and went to pieces with the rest. The great General is one who never loses his form.'[10]

In *The Book of the Happy Warrior* (1918) there is a return to medieval chivalry and the Song of Roland, Richard Coeur de Lion, St. Louis, Robin Hood and the Black Prince. In the Preface, which he directs 'to all Boys', Newbolt sets out the main principles of Chivalry — 'First, service in peace and war, in love and in religion. Secondly, Brotherhood and Equality throughout the Order — whatever their rank or nationality, and whether they were hunting or dining together, or fighting against one another, all knights were brothers. Thirdly a Right Pride — the pride of *parage* not *orgueil*: pride, that is, not in yourself but in your Order. Fourthly, the Consecration of Love; and, Fifthly, the help and Defence of the Weak, the Suffering and the Oppressed.'[11] It would be quite wrong, however, to see in all this simply a sentimental, blimpish, archaic point of view. In a final section on 'Chivalry of To-day' Newbolt shows himself to be forward-looking. He deplores the gulf which developed in late nineteenth century schools between learning and athletics, the training of the mind and the training of the body: far more science should be taught in schools, he urged, and there was a pressing need to destroy class barriers. 'There must be no exclusiveness, no *orgueil*, no looking down upon comrades, no talk of temporary gentlemen.'[12]

Other literary work during the war emphasises Newbolt's versatility. *Aladore* (1914) is a medieval romance written in instalments for *Blackwood's Magazine* and couched in the language of Old England, while *The Story of the Oxfordshire and Buckinghamshire Light Infantry* is a straightforward History of his son's regiment. *The Travelling Companion*, originally a story by Hans Andersen, was written up by Newbolt into an opera to be set to music by C.V. Stanford, not in the event very successfully. Before the war Newbolt had done a great deal to revitalize the Royal Society of Literature, where he was Professor of Poetry, and *A New Study of English Poetry* (1917) contained some of the critical lectures he had delivered at the Society and among them one that advanced a robust defence of the English Ballad. Finally *St. George's Day* (1918) was a book of twelve poems about the war, written in the style of his earliest work. As a poet he professed to be looking for a new formula, but he had not found it yet. In addition to all this he worked for the Intelligence Section of the Admiralty from 1917 onwards, 'writing accounts of the secret events and dodges',[13] as he put it, and preparing a book on the Submarine Campaign. In the winter of 1917 he spent a few days in Scapa Flow on HMS *Hercules*, discussing tactics and keeping himself generally briefed. 'They assume omniscience on my part in naval matters,' he complained, 'which is quite troublesome because I have to guess half the time!'[14] In the last years of the war Lord Beaverbrook persuaded him to take control of the daily All-

World Cable Department, monitoring the cables sent out. While in this job he put forward plans for a wireless service of Imperial News after the War and the scheme was in fact accepted in 1922. 'Rather a big babe', he called it, 'my biggest'.[15]

When the war ended in November 1918 the Newbolt family remained intact — indeed within a month the first grandson was born. The wider family of Cliftonians, however, had not escaped so lightly. Just over 3,000 had served in the war and 578 were dead, many of them very young men. The cricket XI of 1914 certainly 'played the game': all of them fought in the war; five were killed, one died of disease and four were wounded.[16] The school carried on during the war years but it was a grim time, the constant news of losses hanging heavily over masters and boys alike. The number of games fixtures was reduced, economies of fuel, paper and rations were introduced, frills and festivities were discontinued. Sixteen masters were away on military service, eight other masters were bereaved: one of Percival's sons was killed, two of James Wilson's, and one of the serving Headmaster, John King.

Towards the end of 1917 Newbolt attended a meeting of the Old Cliftonian Society in London to discuss the question of a Clifton College War Memorial. *The Cliftonian* magazine reported that 'Sir Henry Newbolt said it had fallen to his lot during the last few years to study the history of the war somewhat intimately, and he had been impressed by the fact, from being brought into contact with a considerable number of those serving in high positions in the Navy, Army, and other public services, that the Public Schools of the country had rendered a service in the war which to a large extent had saved the country. The Public Schools at a critical period of the war supplied something like 30,000 officers, equivalent for an army of 1,000,000 men. They were efficient and splendid leaders. Clifton had taken its full share in the work . . . they had given to the country three distinguished Generals in Sir George Younghusband, Sir William Birdwood, and Sir Douglas Haig.' He might well have added that apart from one Commander-in-Chief and one Army Commander, Clifton also provided 23 Major-Generals and 52 Brigadier-Generals.[18] It was agreed that, in addition to an Endowment Fund, a permanent memorial would be built at Clifton, and *The Cliftonian* of June 1919 carried these verses of Newbolt's intended *For a Memorial*:[19]

From the great Marshal to the last recruit
  These, Clifton, were thyself, thy spirit in deed
Thy flower of chivalry, thy fallen fruit,
  And thine immortal seed.

The Memorial eventually chosen was an Archway, commissioned from the architect Charles Holden who had already designed the much acclaimed Public Library in Bristol. For Sir John Betjeman the new Archway was 'next to the Chapel the most distinguished of the recent additions . . . like all good architecture, it is satisfactory to the eye when seen from any angle.'[20] It was opened by Earl Haig in 1922, the year when he became President of Clifton College and when Newbolt was elected President of the Old Cliftonian Association. 'Courage, manliness, and truth.' Haig said at the ceremony, '.. clean living and honest dealing are the qualities that have made our nation great, and must be preserved if that greatness is to last. Nothing can take their place. Cleverness and skill in Arts and Sciences are much, but they are not enough, if the other qualities are absent.' Newbolt, standing in the crowd, would certainly have agreed with him, as might Percival had he been there: but he had died three years before and lay buried in due state beneath the High Altar of the Chapel.

'My line may be a small one, but fate laid it among great men,' mused Newbolt when he succeeded F.E. Younghusband as Old Cliftonian President.[21] The sentiment was emphasised a few months later when he boarded a Bristol train at Paddington in the company of Haig, Younghusband and J.H. Whitley, Speaker of the House of Commons, all bound for a Council meeting to appoint a new Headmaster of Clifton. Newbolt could not resist the chance to secure details of the final campaigns of 1918 from the ultimate authority. 'He was modest to perfection', he wrote of Haig, 'it was like reading Caesar's Gallic War in which he never speaks in the first person and only once mentions "Caesar". Meanwhile dear old F.E.Y. sat hunched and silent in the corner, with large coal-like eyes. Interesting as the other two were, I couldn't forget that it was he, and not they, who started on that wonderful boyish journey across the illimitable plain of flowers in a Turkestan April morning . . .'[22]

John King had ruled Clifton in difficult times but he left a buoyant school of high repute and flourishing in numbers. 'We feel sure', wrote *The Cliftonian*, 'that under no other Headmaster has there been less discontent or more general cheerfulness in the School.'[23] The first layman to be Headmaster of Clifton would inevitably have been responsible for a change of emphasis, especially in religious affairs: King was certainly no Percival, but in his quiet and friendly way he won great respect and affection from the staff and boys. He was succeeded in 1923 by Norman Whatley, an Oxford classics don who presided over Clifton's fortunes for the rest of Newbolt's lifetime, initiating changes as they seemed necessary, gradually shedding outmoded practices, making the school an expanding, prosperous and civilized place with, especially in the 1930's, a high level of academic success measured in terms of Oxford and Cambridge scholarships. *The Cliftonian* reported in 1931 that at an O.C. dinner the Headmaster 'in a most happy speech almost persuaded the numerous patriarchs present that the prowess of the present School, both in the field and in the form room, was equal, if not superior, to that of the School in their days.'[24]

Newbolt's post-war years were spent occupied by a heavy programme of public work, and by writing. Among the dozen or so books he produced during this period three were boys' adventure stories similar to the ones he had already written. *The Book of the Long Trail* appeared in 1919, *The Book of Good Hunting* in 1920, and *The Book of the Grenvilles* in 1921. The latter is a well-contrived series of time-travel episodes in which the themes of Chivalry and Time and also the question of hereditary characteristics are considered. Tom, Dick, and Harry, three brothers, stay in Oxfordshire with Mr. & Mrs. Diamid whose own sons have been killed in the war. In a discussion on 'Time' Mrs. Diamid explains her husband's view — which is probably Newbolt's own: 'he believes that nothing which really exists ever ceases to exist. He thinks it really worth while to try and place yourself outside Time and get a different view of life.'[25] Virgil's sentiments express this philosophy well, Diamid argues, especially in the words 'Spiritus intus alit' (Clifton's motto of course, chosen by Newbolt's admired teacher Sidney Irwin). The boys try out Diamid's theories on time-travel and are duly swept back into the fourteenth century disputes of Sir Theobald Grenville with the Bishop of Exeter (a figure rather reminiscent of Percival), or the last hours of Sir Richard Grenville of the *Revenge*, or the tragic deaths of the much admired Grenfell brothers on the Western Front. It is an ingenious book, an engrossing blend of philosophy and historical novel.

During the 1920's Newbolt became established as, among other things, a major naval historian. *Submarine and anti-Submarine*, his study of the underwater campaign, was well received when it appeared in 1918 and he followed it with *A Naval History of the War*, published in 1920. In 1923 he was commissioned to write the last two volumes of the *Official Naval*

History of the War and, after a great deal of work, he duly produced Volume IV in 1928 and Volume V in 1931. 'It is quite possible that I shall be attacked from both sides' he wrote to his wife: 'from the Admiralty for not glorifying their Chief, and from the critics for not damning him.' He had a 'strong feeling' for Jellicoe and thought 'his merits were greater than his reward. But the truth is there below the deserved eulogy — the truth that we were saved by the Govt. and not by the High Command . . . it is the lesson of the war.'[26] In fact he thought that April 30th, 1917 was the turning-point in the War; the day Maurice Hankey, Secretary to Lloyd George, persuaded the Cabinet to adopt the convoy system. 'Who won the War?' he asked his wife in a letter, 'A young man you never heard of!'[27]

'I've been, off and on, regretting the seven-and-a-half years I've spent on the Naval History' Newbolt confessed, but 'A man's first duty is to feed his family.'[28] He had also spent a number of years on a series of educational books for Nelson's as well as anthologies and essays in literary criticism. He was always anxious to encourage young poets when he detected their talent, and in his anthology *New Paths on Helicon* (1927) he collected poems by the 'younger generation' with biographical notes which included 'a consideration of the possible result of their work on the future of poetry and thought.' 'It is a work of great vitality' writes the poet Patric Dickinson 'and it shows what a zest and love for poetry Newbolt quite impersonally had.'[29] As for his own work as a poet, the post-war years were plainly a struggle. First, he was too busy with his commissioned writing and various public duties, second he was looking for a new style — 'It is a great thing to write a poem' he wrote in 1926 'and I know I'm going to do that again and again. They'll be none the worse for having waited so long in the chrysalis. My earlier stage was a marked one and it's as well to have got a good way from it before I ask them to receive me in a new spirit — new not to me but to them.'[30] He did actually find this new style in what are quite possibly his two best poems, *The Linnet's Nest* written in 1924 and *The Nightjar*, finished the next year. He is still concerned with Time and Immortality but now looks to the changing seasons of nature, the world of animals and birds. *The Nightjar* is worth quoting in full in case there are any who doubt Newbolt's essential ability as a poet.

> We loved our Nightjar, but she would not stay with us.
> We had found her lying as dead, but soft and warm,
> Under the apple tree beside the old thatched wall.
> Two days we kept her in a basket by the fire,

Fed her, and thought she well might live — till suddenly
In the very moment of most confiding hope
She raised herself all tense, quivered and drooped and died.
Tears sprang into my eyes — why not? the heart of man
Soon sets itself to love a living companion,
The more so if by chance it asks some care of him.
And this one had the sort of loveliness that goes
Far deeper than the optic nerve — full fathom five
To the soul's ocean cave, where Wonder and Reason
Tell their alternate dreams of how the world was made.
So wonderful she was — her wings the wings of night
But powdered here and there with tiny golden clouds
And wave-line markings like sea-ripples on the sand.
O how I wish I might never forget that bird —
Never! But even now, like all beauty of earth,
She is fading from me into the dusk of Time.

Unfortunately, Newbolt found it very difficult to write enough verses that satisfied him now: he was 'writing poems by day and burying them at sunset.' He could not escape from his poetic past, and the patriotic years.

Even in the middle of the War he had written 'Patriotism will be the death of me . . . I deny that there is such a word: I maintain that it should be forbidden.'[31] '*Drake's Drum* was a good poem', he recollected at much the same time and in it 'I did give my country a legend of real value. You needn't add that I also gave it the phrase "Play the game" — I find even blighted foreigners now using it.'[32] Rather like H.M. Stanley who was dogged for the rest of his life by the words he used to greet Livingstone, or the Cliftonian A.E.J. Collins, a modest boy who was constantly embarrassed by being hailed everywhere as the holder of the world record number of runs scored in a cricket match, Newbolt found that 'Play the game', the popular refrain, jangled before him wherever he went. In 1923 he was invited by the Canadian government to be their first Imperial Lecturer and he was enthusiastically received. But 'as for "Play up and play the game", he wrote from Ottawa, 'it's a kind of Frankenstein's Monster that I created thirty years ago and now I find it falling on my neck at every street corner! In vain do I explain what is poetry: they roar for "Play up": they put it on their war memorials and their tombstones: it's their National Anthem.'[33] Uncomfortable though it might be for him, the fact was that Newbolt had become a national symbol, and this Canadian visit proved it.

A family friend wrote to Lady Newbolt 'the echoes of his sojourn in the Western provinces one still hears. I doubt if any visitor from this country ever made such an impression with people of that region. A very new community always values the qualities which Sir Henry possessed, which were the finest qualities that an ancient society can produce.'[34]

Recognition of Newbolt's stature in this respect came in the New Year's Honours list of 1922 when he was made a Companion of Honour. 'I hardly knew what a C.H. was', he commented on hearing the news. 'It is limited to fifty and there are actually twenty-six: its good points are that it was founded for Jan Smuts who didn't want other things . . . finally, it is given for "conspicuous service of National importance." I rather like that.'[35] The honour came to Newbolt not so much as a poet but as a man of affairs: the naval historian and Admiralty adviser, the member of numerous Committees, perhaps the most important of which was the one set up by H.A.L. Fisher, the President of the Board of Education in 1919. This Committee, of which Newbolt was to be Chairman, had the task of reporting to the Government on the position of English in the educational system. The members were not chosen by him yet out of eight men four were Old Cliftonians and one a Clifton Master, J.H. Fowler, the School librarian. The other Cliftonians were Quiller-Couch and F.S. Boas who had sat together in the same classes at Clifton forty years before. The report, most of it couched in Newboltian prose, was greeted enthusiastically by Fisher and might well have revolutionised the teaching of English in schools: but there was a change of Government and it was shelved.

During the 1920's some of the ties with Newbolt's Clifton past were lost. Apart from the death of his mother in 1921, which affected him deeply, there were the deaths of G.F. Wollaston in 1926, and E.M. Oakeley in 1927. His own contemporary J.E. McTaggart died, rather young, in 1925. 'I could have spared all living philosophers if they would only have let me keep McTaggart . . . no one else has enabled me to see through half as much of the brick wall that shuts us in', Newbolt wrote when he heard the news. His own preoccupation with Time had been much influenced throughout his life by his friendship with this splendid mind 'lodged in so funny a dumpling of a head on a sack of a body.' Newbolt understood McTaggart's view to be 'that all real existence is spiritual: Time and Space (matter) are illusions and will pass away: our lives in Time pass away and all lives will pass away when Time ends: but not our life, our personal life, which is eternal . . .'[36] These sentiments, indeed, are the theme of many of Newbolt's writings.

In January 1928 Earl Haig died unexpectedly, of a heart attack. Though they had not known each other well at school, a friendship grew between Haig and Newbolt in later life. Newbolt wrote that it was Haig who took the initiative: 'pleased as I was to find this kind of big brotherly affection putting its arm round my shoulder I was myself surprised, almost puzzled. I think now that among all my confused moods he had seen some reason to think me sympathetic to feelings of his own of which we never spoke. Anyhow, I found in him a religious sense which suited me down to the soles of my soul!'. The great tragedy of Haig's career was that no mutual trust grew between him and the Prime Minister, Lloyd George. It is not perhaps surprising. Haig the professional soldier, the embodiment of honesty, integrity and Christian moral values, tongue-tied in debate, had little in common with one of the most dynamic, opportunistic, fast-thinking, political wits of his generation — except that they were both trying to win a war. So there has always been controversy surrounding Haig's role as Commander-in-Chief: but it is important to distinguish between well-informed criticism and popular myth. For many years now the latter has held sway, fuelled by allegedly inaccurate popular works such as Alan Clark's *The Donkeys* or the musical play *Oh what a Lovely War* which portrays the Field Marshal as little more than a callous buffoon.[38] The verdict of the professional military historians who have studied Haig's campaigns is quite different. Even Liddell Hart, perhaps his sternest critic, readily concedes that 'as a great gentleman, also in the widest sense, and as a pattern of noble character, Haig will stand out in the Roll of History, *chevalier sans peur et sans reproche*, more spotless by far than most of Britain's national heroes. Most of all, perhaps, because in his qualities and defects he was the very embodiment of the national character and the army tradition.' He was, in short, the archetypal Newbolt hero: after all, he had been for five years a Clifton pupil of John Percival, his Headmaster and his Housemaster in School House. Those who seek to know why Haig remained austere, high principled, courageous, and relentlessly dedicated to honourable victory should surely look no further.

The respect which Haig, together with other distinguished pupils of Percival, retained to the end for the message he had so firmly impressed upon them at School is witnessed by a lengthy letter to *The Cliftonian* written by Newbolt just before Haig's death and signed by Haig, Newbolt, Sir Herbert Warren, J.H. Whitley and Sir Francis Younghusband.

'We are Old Cliftonians who left the School long ago', it begins, 'but are still, and more than ever, concerned for its lasting welfare. We remember the great days of Percival and Wilson, and we have since watched with interest and sympathy every development in the history of

Clifton, and every indication of the growth of her power for good. We look with pride on the spirit and success of the younger generations, and we are moved with a strong desire to send them a message out of the past, in the hope that our experience of life may perhaps here and there lighten a difficulty or confirm a faith . . .

'In the last forty or fifty years we have lived through times of great prosperity and still greater danger and anxiety. These years have convinced us all that no kind of life is complete, no kind of life can make the world intelligible or give us any lasting satisfaction, unless there enters into it the element which is called Religion . . . It is our hope that our school may receive in the future a continually more effective equipment for this search; such instruction as helped us in our own youth to recognise that our existence is more than an individual existence . . .'[40]

The Old Cliftonians voted to raise a statue in Haig's memory and the Chairman of the Committee entrusted with this duty was Newbolt's brother, now Sir Francis. There was some talk of an equestrian statue but in the end a standing bronze figure was commissioned from the sculptor W. McMillan. In trench coat and peaked cap, a map spread out upon his knee, the Field Marshal gazes across the Close from the edge of the School House lawn. In the absence of his widow, who was unwell, the statue was unveiled by Haig's young daughter, Lady Alexandra, just after the 1932 Commemoration service. In thanking the Old Cliftonians for providing the statue, the Headmaster observed that it would 'keep before us the memory of a man whose outstanding qualities were endurance, resolution, and every kind of trait involving dignity and courtesy, separated from pettiness and jealousy. No school could ask for more than to send into the world boys in whom these qualities prevailed.'[41] J.H. Whitley, the President of the College, drew upon a more familiar theme: how appropriate the position of the statue was, he remarked, near to Haig's own house, School House, and to the Memorial Gateway which he himself had opened, and looking out over the Close where his earliest battles were fought and won — on the rugby football field.

PART EIGHT: 1928–1938

'Is Time the Master or not?'

The Poet Laureate, Robert Bridges, a man who had befriended and encouraged Newbolt, died in April 1930 and there were many who mentioned Newbolt's name as his successor. But, as he explained to his wife 'I tell them that one look into *Poems New and Old* would convince Ramsay Mac. that I am the last man on whom his choice could fall: and everybody agrees to that. "You see you belong to the wrong generation! In fact to the generation that prepared to defend the country — which is now a crime".' He did not feel disappointed. 'I've written and published in *The Times*, or on public monuments, all the Trafalgar odes and commemorative verses that were wanted . . . It would be a setback to have to do these things all over again on occasions which perhaps wouldn't suit me.'[1]

Instead he embarked upon what was to be his last completed book: the first volume of his autobiography which he entitled, very significantly, *My World as in my Time*. 'I'm always feeling the bitter of the sweet', he complained '— and the unanswerable riddle of Time. Is Time the Master or not?[2] He found it to some extent painful recording the early years of his life for the book: they had been so vivid, so enjoyable. 'When I'm looking back on my life (as I am now) it isn't the wrongs I've done that hurt me so much as the Paradise I've seen and left behind.'[3] Yet it is one of his best pieces of writing; elegant, humorous, modest, wise, wide-ranging in literary, political and social reference. It was published in 1932 and he began the second volume, but never finished it. The remaining fragments of autobiography together with a collection of Newbolt's letters were published under the editorship of his widow in 1942 as *The later Life and Letters of Sir Henry Newbolt*. From 1933 onwards he fell victim to what his wife called 'some insidious enemy microbe': it caused depression and — tragic in so industrious a man — inertia. In 1934 the Newbolts took the brave decision to leave Netherhampton and move back to a small house in London to cut down on travel and be nearer family and friends. Perhaps, too, his spirits would revive. But Newbolt could not shake off his affliction and it rendered him increasingly silent and inactive until he died on April 19th, 1938. On June 10th his ashes were buried at the Island

17 Above: The Unveiling of the South African War Memorial by Lord Methuen on June 25th, 1905.

18 Below: Netherhampton House, near Salisbury, Newbolt's home from 1907 to 1934.

19 Henry Newbolt in 1908, aged 46.

20 A remarkable photograph of the first five Headmasters of Clifton. Left to right: Glazebrook, Percival, King, Wilson, David.

21 Sir Henry Newbolt, c. 1927.

Church at Orchardleigh and his son Francis read aloud one of Newbolt's most moving prose passages, the funeral scene from *The Old Country*.

There was a memorial service in Westminster Abbey, and there were many tributes. Walter de la Mare in *The Times* wrote that 'His deepest, quietest, most precious poems came later.'[5] *The Cliftonian* carried a lengthy article 'by an old schoolfellow' (Couch? Boas?) who wrote 'If he derived, as I think he did, something of a high quality from his Clifton days, and through it honour among men, he undoubtedly reflected back on the school an honour and fame of which we may be proud for all time.'[6] Other tributes recalled his 'oval classical face with its parchment-coloured skin, smooth silvery hair, hawklike nose, small tight-lipped mouth, and eyes now veiled in reveries, now fixed on yours with keen penetrating gaze ... such a face as Virgil's may have been', his love of good food, good wine, good company and, above all, good conversation.[7] 'When I first knew him,' wrote Ralph Furse 'he could be a trifle cocksure, even assertive; and occasionally there were flashes of temper. But in later years he turned all golden mellow like a ripe pear, with sometimes a dry after-taste such as good pears have. At a jest, even if Rabelaisian, his rather severe features would crease themselves into a sustained silent grin of appreciation. But in all matters of taste and conduct he drew the line swiftly and rather sharply.'[8] Many emphasised his capacity for friendship and his liking for young people, warmly reciprocated. He was, as a friend observed, one of those people who understand things without having them explained.[9]

His death came at an anxious time: war again was in the wind and soon to become a sorry fact. Just before it began a new Headmaster, Bertrand Hallward, arrived at Clifton; a tall, fair-haired, vigorous, youthful-looking Cambridge classics don. At first he withstood the pressure to move the school away from Bristol to a safer place and the boys came out of a lecture on November 24th, 1940 to see the heart of the City ablaze from a devastating air attack. On December 2nd another raid scattered bombs in the Clifton area, one landing neatly in the gap between two boys' boarding houses, Polack's and Wiseman's. A move had to be made, for parents were becoming anxious and without new boys there would soon be no school: at short notice a clutch of hotels in the Cornish seaside town of Bude were acquired and there the boys of Clifton repaired to live out the war in safety, reduced in numbers but not — to judge by academic results and the distinguished later careers of many 'Bude' Cliftonians — in vigour. Newbolt's younger brother Sir Francis died in 1940 and in referring to his training as a scientist, his skill as an etcher and his distinction as a lawyer *The Cliftonian* pointed out that: 'Clifton then stood, as it has tried to stand ever since, for a catholicity of intellectual interests and Newbolt's career affords a good example of the width of Clifton training.'[10] The next issue carried a photograph of the memorial tablet dedicated to Henry Newbolt. It displays a portrait head, a representation of *Drake's Drum* with two drumsticks, and the inscription 'Henry Newbolt, Poet 1862–1938, Anima Mundi Sis Memor.' It is to be found today on a pillar at the east end of Clifton Chapel.

'Clifton will never be quite the same again' *The Cliftonian* noted as the school prepared to move back from Bude after VE day.[11] It was true. American troops had used the College buildings during the War and converted Big School into a central dining hall, so individual houses ceased to be responsible for catering arrangements and the intense House rivalry (or 'patriotism') that had been a feature of the pre-war school faded considerably. The hand-to-mouth experiences of Bude led to a breakdown of some of the more formal traditions of Clifton. Not that rural Cornwall had been without its charms. 'Whenever the Close is hushed, as Newbolt wrote', a Bude cricketer mused in 1942, 'we will remember the pleasant small ground where a six went over the cliff and the sun shone blindingly off the sea.'[12] Winston Churchill, not perhaps a hero exactly in the Newbolt mould, visited Clifton in 1946, now no longer Prime Minister. Was the Labour Government a threat to the Public Schools? 'Baffled and perplexed about the future', wrote *The Cliftonian* 'we cling tenaciously to the present.'

Bertrand Hallward left in 1948 to lavish his considerable resources of energy and imagination on the task of converting the Higher Education College at Nottingham into a full-scale University. He was replaced by Desmond Lee whose achievements in six years at Clifton impressed everyone sufficiently for him to be described at a Commemoration Speech in 1954 as 'the greatest Headmaster in the United Kingdom' without too much fear of contradiction.[13] The 300 boys who had returned from Bude swelled to 585 in 1952, with 'great pressure on the entry for the next five or six years at least!'[14] These were times which witnessed visits from Princess Elizabeth and General Omar Bradley, surely a Newbolt paladin, who had formulated plans for the invasion of Normandy in what had been Percival's study in School House. In 1951 there were 18 awards at Oxford and Cambridge and a crowd of between three and four thousand turned up to watch the annual cricket match between Clifton and Tonbridge at Lord's. With the demise of the Labour government in 1951 a new confidence returned together with the Festival of Britain, and in 1952, the 'new Elizabethan age'. Clifton aimed high: 'I have tried to make it clear', said Desmond Lee voicing sentiments worthy of Percival in a sermon shortly before he left to be Headmaster of Winchester 'that to my mind a willingness to tolerate the second-rate is the most tedious and contemptible of vices.'[15]

Under Lee's successors Clifton's material progress has been very marked and the school has been provided with many facilities and increasingly many comforts undreamt of in Newbolt's day. A new Town House opened in 1957 and numbers in the Preparatory School expanded greatly. In the late 1950's it is possible to detect at Clifton the beginning of a critical attitude towards the whole Public School system which was to break out much more widely into the student revolt movement of the next decade. Editors of the School magazine, perhaps egged on by young intellectuals in the Common Room, began to write as early as 1958 that the 'Public School system is now entering its last decade of existence!'[16] There had been much material progress, they conceded, but not enough relaxation of restrictions. Take the School Song, for instance: 'It is perhaps to be expected that those who have known the School Song are unwilling to see it removed even if the present generation regards it as doggerel.'[17] A modest victory was gained in 1961 when it was recorded that at least the verse that contained the line 'the men that tanned the hide of us' is now not sung 'because it contains sentiments unacceptable to modern tastes.'[18] Compulsory Chapel came under heavy fire as well. 'Do we speak of reform?' the Editor enquired, 'Revolution is what we plead for.'[19]

1962 was a memorable year at Clifton, as befitted a Centenary. There were many celebrations, ranging from a Banquet at the Guildhall to a Royal visit. A record number of Oxford and Cambridge Scholarships was achieved. The Headmaster, Nicholas Hammond, left to become Professor of Greek at Bristol University, though not before he had edited and launched a volume entitled *Centenary Essays on Clifton College* containing a number of articles on aspects of Clifton's past. Among them is an essay on Newbolt by John Thorn, Head of the History Department at Clifton and Housemaster of Newbolt's old house, North Town before he left to become successively Headmaster of Repton and Winchester. Thorn accepts that Newbolt was very much affected by the Clifton of his day but for him that implied as many weaknesses as strengths. 'Even in 1924', he writes, 'Newbolt, while no longer extolling the war as magnificent and manly, was seeing it in simple terms as an issue of right and wrong . . . It is not, perhaps, altogether fanciful to blame English Public School education, and Clifton education in particular, for this immaturity in Newbolt's vision.'[20] Nor does he care for Newbolt's attitude to religion.

'He was, . . . , though a God-fearing man and conforming Churchman, suspicious of too much dogma. To him the Christian religion was, primarily, a confirmation of the organic nature of the past and present, of the immortality of the soul; and secondly, a cohesive force in the state . . . With what some consider the true heart of Christianity, its emphasis on the fallen state of man and his need for redemption, with the sacramental life, Newbolt seems to have been little concerned — and here again we see some of the influence of Percival and Wilson, his two great mentors.'[21] Finally, though conceding that he could write 'ballad poetry of a high order that in this last century has only been surpassed by Kipling', Thorn does not really think much of him as a poet. 'We may deny Henry Newbolt a place even on the foothills of English poetry. We may find it difficult to quote "Play up, play up, and play the game" with a wholly straight face. We may recoil at his imperialism. We may find his vague Liberal Christianity a poor lean philosophy in the present battle against materialism.' What, for Thorn, can be salvaged from this wreck? — only Newbolt's vision of the Community, the Brotherhood bound by service to an ideal.[22] After this onslaught even Princess Alexandra's visit and her view that *The Best School of All* was 'a jolly good song' did not do much to retrieve Newbolt's reputation at Clifton.

Yet John Thorn's low opinion of Newbolt the poet was not shared by John Betjeman who wrote in the Introduction to his edition of Newbolt's poems, published in 1940: 'Newbolt's poetry is easy to understand, rhythmical, and full of memorable lines. Because of these qualities and because his earlier poetry is distinctly martial where it is not nostalgic, modern literary people have been inclined to dismiss him as a minor Kipling. Though this has not weakened Newbolt's popular hold, it has been the cause of the neglect of his highly original qualities as a poet. There is really no parallel with Kipling, for Kipling was a great prose writer but not a great poet, and he was never a critic. Newbolt is a better poet than Kipling, and was a severe critic of his own work and an understanding one of that of others.'[23]

By the 1960's the world of 'pop' culture had opened wide and with it the cult of the anti-hero and the protest song took hold. The new idol of schoolboy literature was not a 'Newbolt man'[24] derivative but one to whom sex, money and glamour were at least as important as adventure, and for whom in the pursuit of an admittedly worthy goal, the end usually justified the means. Such was Ian Fleming's creation 'James Bond': a poll taken among Cliftonians in 1964 established that on average each boy had read five James Bond books.[25] The Public Schools have gradually encountered a mounting pressure for change in social patterns and taste and if Newbolt thought that the Clifton of 1922 'was almost incredibly different' from the school he had known, the Clifton of the 1980's might seem incredibly different still. Or would it really? He would still see the 1st XI practising on Bigside, the fine buildings essentially unchanged, the Close richly green in the summer sun. He would still find a reverence for scholarship, an enthusiasm for games and a strong sense of fellowship. And are young men like the School House boy who narrowly escaped death on patrol in Belfast and the Polack's boy who fought for his country in the Israeli army not Newbolt heroes in their own turn?

It is unwise to scoff at Henry Newbolt, especially on the basis of a superficial reading of a few of his most quoted verses. He was a fine man and at his best a good poet, respected on both counts throughout his lifetime. He was not a man swayed by fashion or moved by specious argument. He perceived a Truth and kept to it; for as he well knew, between ultimate Truth and Falsehood, only Time will tell.

THE 'CLIFTON' POEMS

The following poems are the ones
most relevant to Clifton. Nearly all
were published in the volume entitled
Clifton Chapel and other School poems
which was produced in 1908.

Vitaï Lampada*

There's a breathless hush in the Close to-night—
  Ten to make and the match to win—
A bumping pitch and a blinding light,
  An hour to play and the last man in.
And it's not for the sake of a ribboned coat,
  Or the selfish hope of a season's fame,
But his Captain's hand on his shoulder smote—
  'Play up! play up! and play the game!'

The sand of the desert is sodden red,—
  Red with the wreck of a square that broke;—
The Gatling's jammed and the Colonel dead,
  And the regiment blind with dust and smoke.
The river of death has brimmed his banks,
  And England's far, and Honour a name,
But the voice of a schoolboy rallies the ranks:
  'Play up! play up! and play the game!'

This is the word that year by year,
  While in her place the School is set,
Every one of her sons must hear,
  And none that hears it dare forget.
This they all with a joyful mind
  Bear through life like a torch in flame,
And falling fling to the host behind —
  'Play up! play up! and play the game!'

June, 1892

from Lucretius, *De Rerum Natura*, Book 2, line 79 *et quasi cursores vitaï lampada tradunt* — 'and like runners they pass on the torch of life', a reference to a Greek relay race in which the runners carried a lighted torch.

He Fell among Thieves

'Ye have robbed', said he, 'ye have slaughtered and made an end,
   Take your ill-got plunder, and bury the dead:
What will ye more of your guest and sometime friend?'
   'Blood for our blood', they said.

He laughed: 'If one may settle the score for five,
   I am ready; but let the reckoning stand till day:
I have loved the sunlight as dearly as any alive.'
   'You shall die at dawn', said they.

He flung his empty revolver down the slope,
   He climbed alone to the Eastward edge of the trees;
All night long in a dream untroubled of hope
   He brooded, clasping his knees.

He did not hear the monotonous roar that fills
   The ravine where the Yassin river sullenly flows;
He did not see the starlight on the Laspur hills,
   Or the far Afghan snows.

He saw the April noon on his books aglow,
   The wistaria trailing in at the window wide;
He heard his father's voice from the terrace below
   Calling him down to ride.

He saw the gray little church across the park,
   The mounds that hide the loved and honoured dead;
The Norman arch, the chancel softly dark,
   The brasses black and red.

He saw the School Close, sunny and green,
   The runner beside him, the stand by the parapet wall,
The distant tape, and the crowd roaring between
   His own name over all.

He saw the dark wainscot and timbered roof,
   The long tables, and the faces merry and keen;
The College Eight and their trainer dining aloof,
   The Dons on the daïs serene.

He watched the liner's stem ploughing the foam,
  He felt her trembling speed and the thrash of her screw;
He heard her passengers' voices talking of home,
  He saw the flag she flew.

And now it was dawn. He rose strong on his feet,
  And strode to his ruined camp below the wood;
He drank the breath of the morning cool and sweet;
  His murderers round him stood.

Light on the Laspur hills was broadening fast,
  The blood-red snow-peaks chilled to a dazzling white:
He turned, and saw the golden circle at last,
  Cut by the Eastern height.

'O glorious Life, Who dwellest in earth and sun,
  I have lived, I praise and adore Thee.'
                                    A sword swept.

Over the pass the voices one by one
  Faded, and the hill slept.

                                    September 1897

Clifton Chapel

This is the Chapel: here, my son,
  Your father thought the thoughts of youth,
And heard the words that one by one
  The touch of Life has turned to truth.
Here in a day that is not far
  You too may speak with noble ghosts
Of manhood and the vows of war
  You made before the Lord of Hosts.

To set the cause above renown,
  To love the game beyond the prize,
To honour, while you strike him down,
  The foe that comes with fearless eyes;

To count the life of battle good,
    And dear the land that gave you birth,
And dearer yet the brotherhood
    That binds the brave of all the earth—

My son, the oath is yours: the end
    Is His, Who built the world of strife,
Who gave His children Pain for friend,
    And Death for surest hope of life.
To-day and here the fight's begun,
    Of the great fellowship you're free;
Henceforth the School and you are one,
    And what You are, the race shall be.

God send you fortune: yet be sure,
    Among the lights that gleam and pass,
You'll live to follow none more pure
    Than that which glows on yonder brass:
'*Qui procul hinc*', the legend's writ,—
    The frontier-grave is far away—
'*Qui ante diem periit:*
    Sed miles, sed pro patria.'

The Echo

Of a Ballad sung by H. Plunket Greene to his old School

Twice three hundred boys were we,
    Long ago, long ago,
Where the Downs look out to the Severn Sea.
    Clifton for aye!
We held by the game and hailed the team,
For many could play where few could dream.
    City of Song shall stand alway.

Some were for profit and some for pride,
    Long ago, long ago,
Some for the flag they lived and died.

Clifton for aye!
The work of the world must still be done,
And minds are many though truth be one.
  City of Song shall stand alway.

But a lad there was to his fellows sang,
  Long ago, long ago,
And soon the world to his music rang.
  Clifton for aye!
Follow your Captains, crown your Kings,
But what will ye give to the lad that sings?
  City of Song shall stand alway.

For the voice ye hear is the voice of home,
  Long ago, long ago,
And the voice of Youth with the world to roam.
  Clifton for aye!
The voice of passion and human tears,
And the voice of the vision that lights the years.
  City of Song shall stand alway.

The Best School of All

It's good to see the School we knew,
  The land of youth and dream,
To greet again the rule we knew
  Before we took the stream:
Though long we've missed the sight of her,
  Our hearts may not forget;
We've lost the old delight of her,
  We keep her honour yet.

We'll honour yet the School we knew,
  The best School of all:
We'll honour yet the rule we knew,
  Till the last bell call.
For, working days or holidays,
And glad or melancholy days,

They were great days and jolly days
    At the best School of all.

The stars and sounding vanities
    That half the crowd bewitch,
What are they but inanities
    To him that treads the pitch?
And where's the wealth, I'm wondering,
    Could buy the cheers that roll
When the last charge goes thundering
    Beneath the twilight goal?

The men that tanned the hide of us,
    Our daily foes and friends,
They shall not lose their pride of us
    Howe'er the journey ends.
Their voice, to us who sing of it,
    No more its message bears,
But the round world shall ring of it
    And all we are be theirs.

To speak of Fame a venture is,
    There's little here can bide,
But we may face the centuries,
    And dare the deepening tide:
For though the dust that's part of us
    To dust again be gone,
Yet here shall beat the heart of us—
    The School we handed on!

We'll honour yet the School we knew,
    The best School of all:
We'll honour yet the rule we knew,
    Till the last bell call.
For, working days or holidays,
And glad or melancholy days,
They were great days and jolly days
    At the best School of all.

March 19, 1899

The Schoolfellow

Our game was his but yesteryear;
  We wished him back; we could not know
The self-same hour we missed him here
  He led the line that broke the foe.

Blood-red behind our guarded posts
  Sank as of old the dying day;
The battle ceased; the mingled hosts
  Weary and cheery went their way:

'Tomorrow well may bring', we said,
  'As fair a fight, as clear a sun.'
Dear lad, before the word was sped,
  For evermore thy goal was won.

                              November 10, 1899

The School at War

All night before the brink of death
  In fitful sleep the army lay,
For through the dream that stilled their breath
  Too gauntly glared the coming day.

But we, within whose blood there leaps
  The fulness of a life as wide
As Avon's water where he sweeps
  Seaward at last with Severn's tide,

We heard beyond the desert night
  The murmur of the fields we knew,
And our swift souls with one delight
  Like homing swallows Northward flew.

We played again the immortal games,
   And grappled with the fierce old friends,
And cheered the dead undying names,
   And sang the song that never ends;

Till, when the hard, familiar bell
   Told that the summer night was late,
Where long ago we said farewell,
   We said farewell by the old gate.

'O Captains unforgot', they cried,
   'Come you again or come no more,
Across the world you keep the pride,
   Across the world we mark the score.'

May 21, 1901

Commemoration

I sat by the granite pillar, and sunlight fell
   Where the sunlight fell of old,
And the hour was the hour my heart remembered well,
   And the sermon rolled and rolled
As it used to roll when the place was still unhaunted,
   And the strangest tale in the world was still untold.

And I knew that of all this rushing of urgent sound
   That I so clearly heard,
The green young forest of saplings clustered round
   Was heeding not one word:
Their heads were bowed in a still serried patience
   Such as an angel's breath could never have stirred.

For some were already away to the hazardous pitch,
   Or lining the parapet wall,
And some were in glorious battle, or great and rich,

Or throned in a college hall:
And among the rest was one like my own young phantom,
　Dreaming for ever beyond my utmost call.

'O Youth,' the preacher was crying, 'deem not thou
　Thy life is thine alone;
Thou bearest the will of the ages, seeing how
　They built thee bone by bone,
And within thy blood the Great Age sleeps sepulchred
　Till thou and thine shall roll away the stone.

'Therefore the days are coming when thou shalt burn
　With passion whitely hot;
Rest shall be rest no more; thy feet shall spurn
　All that thy hand hath got;
And One that is stronger shall gird thee, and lead thee swiftly
　Whither, O heart of Youth, thou wouldest not.'

And the School passed; and I saw the living and dead
　Set in their seats again,
And I longed to hear them speak of the word that was said,
　But I knew that I longed in vain.
And they stretched forth their hands, and the wind of the spirit took
　　　　　　　　　　　　　　　　　　　them
　Lightly as drifted leaves on an endless plain.

　　　　　　　　　　　　　　　　　　　July 7, 1901

Epistle

To Colonel Francis Edward Younghusband

Across the Western World, the Arabian Sea,
The Hundred Kingdoms and the Rivers Three,
Beyond the rampart of Himálayan snows,
And up the road that only Rumour knows,

Unchecked, old friend, from Devon to Thibet,
Friendship and Memory dog your footsteps yet.

Let not the scornful ask me what avails
So small a pack to follow mighty trails:
Long since I saw what difference must be
Between a stream like you, a ditch like me.

This drains a garden and a homely field
Which scarce at times a living current yield;
The other from the high lands of his birth
Plunges through rocks and spurns the pastoral earth,
Then settling silent to his deeper course,
Draws in his fellows to augment his force,
Becomes a name, and broadening as he goes,
Gives power and purity wher'er he flows,
Till, great enough for any commerce grown,
He links all nations while he serves his own.

Soldier, explorer, statesman, what in truth
Have you in common with homekeeping youth?
'Youth' comes your answer like an echo faint;
And youth it was that made us first acquaint.
Do you remember when the Downs were white
With the March dust from highways glaring bright,
How you and I, like yachts that toss the foam,
From Penpole Fields came stride and stride for home?
One grimly leading, one intent to pass,
Mile after mile we measured road and grass,
Twin silent shadows, till the hour was done,
The shadows parted and the stouter won.
Since then I know one thing beyond appeal—
How runs from stem to stern a trimbuilt keel.
Another day — but that's not mine to tell,
The man in front does not observe so well;
Though, spite of all these five-and-twenty years,
As clear as life our schoolday scene appears.
The guarded course, the barriers and the rope;
The runners, stripped of all but shivering hope;
The starter's good gray head; the sudden hush;

The stern white line; the half-unconscious rush;
The deadly bend, the pivot of our fate;
The rope again; the long green level straight;
The lane of heads, the cheering half unheard;
The dying spurt, the tape, the judge's word.

You, too, I doubt not, from your Lama's hall
Can see the Stand above the worn old wall,
Where then they clamoured as our race we sped,
Where now they number our heroic dead.
As clear as life you, too, can hear the sound
Of voices once for all by 'lock-up' bound,
And see the flash of eyes still nobly bright
But in the 'Bigside scrimmage' lost to sight.

Old loves, old rivalries, old happy times,
These well may move your memory and my rhymes;
These are the Past; but there is that, my friend,
Between us two, that has nor time nor end.
Though wide apart the lines our fate has traced
Since those far shadows of our boyhood raced,
In the dim region all men must explore—
The mind's Thibet, where none has gone before—
Rounding some shoulder of the lonely trail
We met once more, and raised a lusty hail.

'Forward!' cried one, 'for us no beaten track,
No city continuing, no turning back:
The past we love not for its being past,
But for its hope and ardour forward cast:
The victories of our youth we count for gain
Only because they steeled our hearts to pain,
And hold no longer even Clifton great
Save as she schooled our wills to serve the State.
Nay, England's self, whose thousand-year-old name
Burns in our blood like ever-smouldering flame,
Whose Titan shoulders as the world are wide
And her great pulses like the Ocean tide,
Lives but to bear the hopes we shall not see—
Dear mortal Mother of the race to be.'

Thereto you answered, 'Forward! in God's name:
I own no lesser law, no narrower claim.
A freeman's Reason well might think it scorn
To toil for those who may be never born,
But for some Cause not wholly out of ken,
Some all-directing Will that works with men,
Some Universal under which may fall
The minor premiss of our effort small;
In Whose unending purpose, though we cease,
We find our impulse and our only peace.'

So passed our greeting, till we turned once more,
I to my desk and you to rule Indore.
To meet again — ah! when? Yet once we met,
And to one dawn our faces still are set.

September 10, 1904

For a Memorial

1899–1902

CLIFTON, remember these thy sons who fell
    Fighting far over sea:
For they in a dark hour remembered well
    Their warfare learned of thee.

For a War Memorial

CLIFTON COLLEGE, 1914–1918

From the great Marshal to the last recruit
    These, Clifton, were thyself, thy spirit in deed,
Thy flower of chivalry, thy fallen fruit
    And thine immortal seed.

BIBLIOGRAPHY

A. Works by Sir Henry Newbolt (poetry marked *)

Taken from the enemy (Chatto and Windus) 1892
Mordred, a Tragedy (T. Fisher Unwin) 1895
*Admirals All (Elkin Matthews) 1897
*The Island Race (Elkin Matthews) 1898
Stories from Froissart (Macmillan) 1899
Froissart in Britain (J. Nisbet) 1900
*The Sailing of the Longships (Murray) 1902
Songs of the Sea (Boosey, Stainer and Bell) 1904
The Year of Trafalgar (Murray) 1905
The Old Country (Smith Elder, Murray) 1906
*Collected Poems 1907
*Clifton Chapel and other School poems 1908
The New June (Smith Elder, Murray) 1909
*The Book of Cupid (with Lady Hylton) 1909
*Goodchild's Garland (Elkin Matthews) 1909
*Songs of Memory and Hope (Murray) 1909
*Songs of the Fleet (Boosey, Stainer and Bell) 1910
The Twymans (Blackwood) 1911
*Poems New and Old (Murray) 1912
The Book of the Blue Sea (Longmans) 1914
Aladore (Blackwood) 1914
The Book of the Thin Red Line (Longmans) 1915
The Story of the Oxfordshire and Buckinghamshire Light Infantry (Country Life) 1915
Tales of the Great War (Longmans) 1916
The Travelling Companion (Opera, Sir C.V. Stanford) (Stainer and Bell) 1916
The Book of the Happy Warrior (Longmans) 1917
A New Study of English Poetry (Constable) 1917
*St George's Day (Murray) 1918
Submarine and anti-submarine (Longmans) 1918
The Book of the Long Trail (Longmans) 1919
The Book of Good Hunting (Longmans) 1920
A Naval History of the War (Hodder and Stoughton) 1920
An English Anthology of Prose and Poetry (Dent) 1921
The Book of the Grenvilles (Longmans) 1921
Sea Life in English Literature (Nelson) 1925
Studies Green and Gray (Nelson) 1926
New Paths on Helicon (Nelson) 1927
Naval Operations (Official Naval History of the War, Vol IV 1928, Vol V 1931)
My World as in my Time (Faber and Faber) 1932

A Perpetual Memory and other poems (Murray) 1939
The Later Life and Letters of Sir Henry Newbolt (ed. Margaret Newbolt) (Faber) 1942

B. Clifton College Records

The Cliftonian Magazine 1867–1985 (46 volumes)
Clifton College Register 1862–1880 (ed. E.M. Oakeley)
Clifton College Annals and Register 1862–1925 (ed. F. Borwick)
Clifton College Register 1862–1947 (ed. J.A.O. Muirhead)
Clifton Colege Register 1862–1962 (ed. S.P. Beachcroft)
Clifton College Register 1862–1978 (ed. J.B. Evans)

C. Secondary Sources

Betjeman, John (ed.), *Selected Poems of Henry Newbolt* (Nelson) 1940
Birdwood, Lord, *Khaki and Gown, an Autobiography* (Ward Lock) 1941
Birkenhead, Lord, *Rudyard Kipling* (Weidenfeld and Nicolson) 1978
Brittain, F., *Arthur Quiller-Couch, a biographical study of Q* (Cambridge) 1947
Christie, O.F., *Clifton Schooldays* 1879–1885 (Shaylor) 1930
—— *A History of Clifton College* 1860–1934 (Arrowsmith) 1935
Cooper, Duff, *Haig* (Faber and Faber) Vol I 1935, Vol II 1936
David, A.A., *Life and the Public Schools* (Maclehose) 1932
Dickinson, Patric (ed.), *Selected Poems of Henry Newbolt* (Hodder and Stoughton) 1981
Ensor, R.C.K., *England 1870–1914* (Oxford)
Firth, Sir C.H., *T.W. Dunn*
Fowler, T., *The History of Corpus Christi College* 1893
Girouard, Mark, *The Return to Camelot* (Yale University Press) 1981
Graham, G.S., *A Concise History of the British Empire* (Book Club) 1972
Grosskurth, Phyllis, *The Memoirs of John Addington Symonds* (Hutchinson) 1984
Hammond, N.G.L. (ed.), *Centenary Essays on Clifton College* 1962
Henley, W.E. (ed.), *The Collected Poems of T.E. Brown* (Macmillan) 1909
Hinchcliffe, Edgar, *Appleby Grammar School — from Chantry to Comprehensive* (Appleby) 1974
Howarth, Patrick, *Play up and Play the Game* (Eyre Methuen) 1973
Howson, A.G., *A History of Mathematics Education in England* (Cambridge) 1982
Irwin, S.T. (ed.), *Letters of T.E. Brown* (Constable) 1900
—— Clifton School Addresses (Macmillan) 1912
Liddell Hart, B.H., *Reputations* (Murray) 1928
McGarvie, Michael, *Sir Henry Newbolt and Orchardleigh* 1985
Magnus, Laurie, *Herbert Warren of Magdalen, President and Friend 1853–1930* (Murray) 1932
Mozley, J.R., *Clifton Memories* (Arrowsmith) 1927
Morris, James, *Pax Britannica* (Penguin) 1980
Newbolt, Sir F.G., *Clifton College 25 Years Ago, The diary of a Fag* (Robinson) 1904
—— *Clifton College 40 Years Ago, The diary of a Praepostor* (Philip Allan) 1924
Plunket Greene, Harry, *Where the Bright Waters meet* (Witherby) 1969
Quiller-Couch, Sir A., *Memories and Opinions* (Cambridge) 1944
—— (ed.), *T.E. Brown, A Memorial Volume* (Cambridge) 1930
Seaver, George, *Francis Younghusband* 1952

Sixsmith, E.K.G., *Douglas Haig* (Weidenfeld and Nicolson) 1976

Temple, William, *Life of Bishop Percival* (Macmillan) 1921

Terraine, John, *Douglas Haig, the educated soldier* (Hutchinson) 1963

Tompkins, J.C.H., *Clifton at Bude and Butcombe* (Arrowsmith) 1945

Wilson, James M., *An Autobiography 1836–1931* (Sidgwick and Jackson) 1932

Wollaston, A.F.R., *Letters and Diaries*, ed. M. Wollaston (Cambridge) 1933

Woolf, Virginia, *Roger Fry, A Biography* (Hogarth Press) 1940

Younghusband, Sir F.E., *The Light of Experience* (Constable) 1927

REFERENCES

Most of the references and quotations in this book come from three sources — 45 volumes of *The Cliftonian* magazine (abbreviated to C); *My World as in my Time* (abbreviated to MW), Newbolt's first volume of autobiography; and *The Later Life and Letters of Sir Henry Newbolt* (abbreviated to LL). With other sources only the name of the author is normally given, together with the page reference. Full details of the publications will be found in the Bibliography. In the case of a quotation from one of Newbolt's books, only the title is given.

Part 1
1 C Vol 27 p 165
2 C Vol 26 p 128
3 *Clifton College Annals and Register* 1925 p xvii
4 Register 1925 p xix
5 Register 1925 p xx
6 W. Temple *Life of Bishop Percival* p 11
7 Register 1925 p xx
8 *The Twymans* p 99
9 Register 1925 p xxii
10 MW p 7
11 MW p 26
12 MW p 36
13 *The Twymans* p 53

Part 2
1 *The Twymans* p 82
2 W. Temple p 37
3 *The Twymans* p 125
4 MW p 86
5 W. Temple p 351
6 W. Temple p 29
7 MW p 64
8 MW p 66

9 W. Temple p 17
10 F. Newbolt *Diary of a Praepostor* p 149
11 A. Quiller-Couch *Memories and Opinions* pp 61, 62
12 HJN in the Preface to *Letters and Diaries of A.F.R. Wollaston*
13 MW p 49
14 LL p 336
15 C Vol 23 p 53
16 MW p 50
17 W.E. Henley (ed) *The Collected Poems of T.E. Brown* p 78
18 MW p 52
19 C. Firth *T.W. Dunn* p 12
20 MW p 51
21 MW p 51
21 MW p 53
22 MW p 62
23 F. Newbolt *Diary of a Fag* p 125
24 MW p 64
25 A. Quiller-Couch pp 62, 63
26 C Vol 26 p 187
27 MW p 63
28 C Vol 6 p 253
29 F. Newbolt *Diary of a Praepostor* p 126

References

30 LL p 275
31 *Epistle* 1904
32 MW p 77
33 O.F. Christie *Clifton Schooldays* pp 19, 20, 34, 35
34 MW p 61
35 MW p 62
36 C Vol 7 pp 40–47
37 MW p 58
38 C Vol 15 p 299
39 Roger Fry, quoted in Virginia Woolf *Roger Fry, a Biography* pp 33, 35
40 Ibid p 34
41 C Vol 5 pp 428–461
42 MW p 67
43 MW p 68
44 A.G. Howson *A History of Mathematics Education in England* p 133
45 MW p 71
46 LL p 225
47 MW p 84
48 MW p 84

Part 3

1 T. Fowler *The History of Corpus Christi College* p 417
2 *The Twymans* pp 156, 157
3 MW p 108
4 MW p 85
5 MW p 114
6 *The Twymans* p 209
7 MW p 105
8 MW p 110
9 MW p 140
10 *The Twymans* p 136
11 MW p 90
12 MW p 115
13 MW p 115
14 MW p 94
15 *Clifton College Register* 1948 p 44
16 MW p 95
17 F. Newbolt *Diary of a Praepostor* p 89

18 MW p 141
19 MW p 94
20 *The Twymans* p 153

Part 4

1 MW p 154
2 MW p 154
3 MW p 165
4 MW p 167
5 MW p 180
6 *Taken from the Enemy* p 108
7 Ibid p 115
8 R.C.K. Ensor *England 1870–1914* p 232
9 MW p 187
10 Patric Dickinson *Selected Poems of Henry Newbolt* p 18
11 James Morris *Pax Britannica* p 22
12 MW pp 197, 203
13 MW p 204
14 C Vol 15 p 298
15 C Vol 15 pp 370, 371
16 MW p 204
17 C Vol 13 p 175
18 C Vol 15 p 130
19 O.F. Christie *History of Clifton College* p 143
20 C Vol 10 p 89
21 O.F. Christie p 117
22 Ibid p 141
23 C Vol 12 pp 317, 319
24 C Vol 16 p 422

Part 5

1 MW p 196
2 MW p 208
3 *Stories from Froissart* p xxvii
4 MW p 240
5 Patric Dickinson *Selected Poems of Henry Newbolt* p 19
6 MW p 284
7 MW p 242

8 G.S. Graham *A Concise History of the British Empire* p 242
9 MW p 249
10 C Vol 16 p 159
11 O.F. Christie *A History of Clifton College* p 147
12 C Vol 16 p 266
13 C Vol 17 p 349
14 C Vol 17 pp 377, 378
15 C Vol 18 p 128
16 C Vol 18 p 194
17 MW p 252
18 C Vol 18 p 262

Part 6
1 MW p 298
2 MW p 311
3 C Vol 17 p 311
4 C Vol 18 p 97
5 C Vol 18 p 104
6 C Vol 19 p 238
7 O.F. Christie *A History of Clifton College* p 160
8 C Vol 19 p 236
9 C Vol 20 p 68
10 C Vol 21 p 145
11 LL p 80
12 LL p 87
13 Ralph Furse in Introduction to *A Perpetual Memory* p xi
14 LL p 123
15 LL p 131
16 C Vol 22 p 337
17 C Vol 22 p 346
18 C Vol 22 p 377

Part 7
1 LL p 174
2 LL p 190
3 LL p 191
4 LL p 255
5 LL p 200

6 *The Book of the Thin Red Line* p vi
7 *Tales of the Great War* p 1
8 Ibid p 23
9 Ibid p 146
10 Ibid p 169
11 *The Book of the Happy Warrior* p vi
12 Ibid p 276
13 LL p 237
14 LL p 242
15 LL p 256
16 O.F. Christie *A History of Clifton College* p 183
17 C Vol 25 p 165
18 O.F. Christie *A History of Clifton College* p 190
19 C Vol 26 p 6
20 N.G.L. Hammond (ed) *Centenary Essays on Clifton College* p 27
21 LL p 288
22 LL p 292
23 C Vol 28 p 34
24 C Vol 32 p 144
25 *The Book of the Grenvilles* p 38
26 LL p 372
27 LL p 354
28 LL p 374
29 Dickinson p 25
30 LL p 344
31 LL p 222
32 LL p 224
33 LL p 300
34 LL p 300
35 LL p 287
36 LL p 323
37 LL p 355
38 See E.K.G. Sixsmith *Douglas Haig* p 188
39 B.H. Liddell Hart *Reputations* p 123
40 C 30 p 178
41 C 32 p 310
42 C 32 p 308

References

Part 8

 1 LL p 364
 2 LL p 383
 3 LL p 383
 4 Dickinson p 25
 5 C Vol 35 p 249
 6 C Vol 35 p 250
 7 Ralph Furse in the Introduction to *A Perpetual Memory* p xiii
 8 Ibid
 9 LL p 158
10 C Vol 36 p 413
11 C Vol 37 p 286
12 C Vol 37 p 98
13 C Vol 40 p 157
14 C Vol 40 p 4
15 C Vol 40 p 162
16 C Vol 41 p 245
17 C Vol 41 p 233
18 C Vol 42 p 44
19 C Vol 42 p 1
20 N.G.L. Hammond (ed) *Centenary Essays on Clifton College* p 161
21 Ibid p 165
22 Ibid p 167
23 John Betjeman (ed) *Selected poems of Henry Newbolt* 1940 p xiv
24 See Patrick Howarth *Play up and Play the Game* pp 1–14
25 C Vol 43 p 10

INDEX

Index